W9-CZL-750

architecture research office

GRAHAM FOUNDATION | PRINCETON ARCHITECTURAL PRESS series

New Voices in Architecture

presents first monographs on emerging designers from around the world

aro architecture research office

Stephen Cassell | *Adam Yarinsky*

GRAHAM FOUNDATION FOR ADVANCED STUDIES IN THE FINE ARTS, CHICAGO

PRINCETON ARCHITECTURAL PRESS, NEW YORK

For Amy, Will, and Anna—A.Y.   For Alexa and Julia—S.C.

contents

acknowledgments

WE ARE FORTUNATE to have spent several years working in the office of Steven Holl. In this inspiring place we learned that it is possible to unite concept, material, and experience to make an architecture of cultural consequence.

We value the friendship, wit, and perceptive eye of Mayer Rus, an early supporter who continues to be an advocate for our work and that of other emerging designers. From early on in our practice, Paul Warchol has helped us document our work with his beautiful photographs while Judith Nasatir has generously given her time, insight, and editorial skill.

Princeton Architectural Press, under Kevin Lippert's direction, has defined quality publications about architecture and design, and we are proud to be included in this collection. We especially appreciate Clare Jacobson and Nicola Bednarek's editorial guidance in creating this book. We thank Stan Allen, Philip Nobel, Guy Nordenson, and Sarah Whiting for helping to frame our work through their texts. Alexa Mulvihill designed this book with elegance and clarity, and we are thankful for her expertise. In our office, Landry Smith and Kim Yao's diligent efforts and critical eyes successfully guided this project.

We thank our clients, without whom our work would not exist. We appreciate the insight and guidance of the engineers and other consultants with whom we have collaborated. We have also been fortunate to work with excellent contractors and fabricators, who have executed each project with care and skill.

Finally, thank you to everyone who has contributed their talent and energy to ARO, including current staff Ralph Cottiers, Reid Freeman, Ben Fuqua, Beth Huck, Megan Kelly-Sweeney, Josh Pulver, Eunice Seng, Megumi Tamanaha, and Kim Yao.

Stephen Cassell and Adam Yarinsky
New York City, September 2002

preface

introduction

WE HAVE ALWAYS CONSIDERED our office to be a design project in itself, a collaborative enterprise to shape and adjust as it evolves. In this respect, this book serves two functions. First, it documents our body of work. Secondly, it serves as a tool that allows us to reflect on our intentions and our methodology. The seven projects presented here demonstrate the diversity of work within our office, and illustrate both the projects themselves and our working process. In addition to photographs and renderings of each project we have included drawings, models, and sketches from the design process. The images, selected out of hundreds of items, highlight key aspects or moments in each project's development. With this documentation and the four essays by our colleagues we hope to inform the reader about our methods and our work. In turn, we are given the opportunity to reflect, educate ourselves, and adjust how we make architecture.

framework

A few shared basic beliefs about the context of architecture underlie all of our work. We acknowledge that all architecture is situated within a complex system—buildings exist within an elaborate web of relationships. These relationships, whether spatial, material, programmatic, or temporal, are always too intricate to fully know or predict. Similar to the ecology of a forest, or the economics of a small city, certain aspects can be understood; the whole system, however, can never be fully controlled. This complexity has a profound effect on design, which is compounded by the fact that the implementation of architecture is the result of countless decisions made by multiple parties over an extended period of time. In recognition of this fact, we develop strategies through careful study of the specific conditions that surround a project, taking into account the entire system with its complexity and reframing the goals of the project in these terms.

We believe ideas in architecture become manifest through the use of a building and through the relationship it creates to its context. This is in opposition to the concept of designing architecture that serves as an object or a representation of an idea. In order to achieve our objective, the ideas or goals of each project must be clearly stated and conform to one's intuitive experience. Each idea must have direct architectural consequences. Each concept must be logical and consistent to itself, to the goals of the project, and to the world. Our task is to link our ideas and concepts with the specific conditions of each project through the making of architecture.

methodology

Our methodology arises from an insistence on developing, testing, and implementing our architecture based on its underlying ideas. Methodology does not, however, undermine intuition. On the contrary, it serves as a framework in which we can define and test intuitive ideas and in which intuition can flourish. As such, methodology leads to "informed intuition"—once we have produced twenty perspectives of the same conditions, we gain deeper insight into the issues at hand.

To make architecture that is strengthened by its circumstances, we try to understand the complex parameters of each project, and the relationships sustained between it and its context. We start by investigating the project's physical, economic, and social contexts. We study the physical qualities of the site, including climate, topography, and views. We question and define any economic limitations. We consider whom the project is for, what building systems are appropriate to the place, how the project will be implemented, and who will build it. All of this data informs our understanding and helps define a strategy for the creation and implementation of the design.

We begin designing by quickly looking at a broad range of possible design solutions. While we may initially bring a specific set of intentions to a project, we try

3

multiple configurations, usually twenty to thirty test fits, of the program on the site. Unburdened by a singular a priori idea, this early and direct engagement gives us better insight into the basic architectural issues. At the same time we produce a variety of formal solutions to the project. This gathering of information and questioning of the broad context of the project culminate in a series of diagrams that serve to clarify the goals of the project.

We then test specific ways to reach these objectives through architecture. Using drawings, models, and full-size mock-ups we study different options. If one or more of the early schemes is successful, we start an iterative process, experimenting with variations of the proposed idea. These studies start with broad pragmatic and formal strategies. As the design begins to take shape, we focus on different areas and aspects of it in more detail, constantly working in an iterative manner. It is important not to understate the range and intensity of research at this stage, which usually involves studying hundreds of variations, working in models, computer models, and perspectives. As we proceed to hone the architecture, we look for a formal and material language that resonates with the ideas of the project. This is also why our work's language varies from project to project. Each is specific to and consistent with its own conditions and not the result of a superimposed vocabulary. Once this formal, material, and pragmatic logic is set, a whole series of implications becomes evident and drives the design forward. The iterative approach continues throughout the design process, becoming increasingly specific as the project develops. It is through this way of working that ideas are tested against the particular conditions of the project. Often several strategies or ideas coexist within a project, working toward a unified design.

Throughout the design process it is important that the nature of the tools we use be appropriate to the specific problem that is being studied. Therefore we vary the media (scale model, computer model, full-size mock-up) and the vantage point (section, perspective, plan) as well as the level of detail with which we study the design. Speed of feedback is critical to keep it fresh and moving forward. If too much detail or time is invested in one particular drawing or model, design may stagnate, and one may hesitate to try alternatives.

Through our work we desire to learn and to make better architecture. While we do bring a particular viewpoint to each project, we do not presume to know the answer before we start working. By gathering information, rigorously trying alternatives at every stage, and gradually pushing forward in an iterative way, our intuition is bolstered by experience. Ultimately, we strive to find an elegant solution to the problem at hand, a resonance between ideas and forms that communicates directly to the user. The success of each project can only be measured through its use and the relationships it fosters. In the end, the work stands by itself.

ARO's Applied Research

Stan Allen

¹**re·search** \ri-'sərch, 'rē-,\ *n* [MF *recerche*, fr. *recerchier* to investigate thoroughly, fr. OF, fr. *re- + cerchier* to search — more at SEARCH] (1577) **1** : careful or diligent search **2** : studious inquiry or examination; *esp* : investigation or experimentation aimed at the discovery and interpretation of facts, revision of accepted theories or laws in the light of new facts, or practical application of such new or revised theories or laws **3** : the collecting of information about a particular subject
²**research** *vt* (1593) **1** : to search or investigate exhaustively ⟨∼ a problem⟩ **2** : to do research for ⟨∼ a book⟩ ∼ *vi* : to engage in research

¹**prac·tice** *or* **prac·tise** \'prak-təs\ *vb* **prac·ticed** *or* **prac·tised; prac·tic·ing** *or* **prac·tis·ing** [ME *practisen*, fr. MF *practiser*, fr. *practique, pratique* practice, n., fr. LL *practice*, fr. Gk *praktikē*, fr. fem. of *praktikos*] *vt* (14c) **1 a** : CARRY OUT, APPLY ⟨∼ what you preach⟩ **b** : to do or perform often, customarily, or habitually ⟨∼ politeness⟩ **c** : to be professionally engaged in ⟨∼ medicine⟩ **2 a** : to perform or work at repeatedly so as to become proficient ⟨∼ the act⟩ **b** : to train by repeated exercises ⟨∼ pupils in penmanship⟩ **3** *obs* : PLOT ∼ *vi* **1** : to do repeated exercises for proficiency **2** : to pursue a profession actively **3** *archaic* : INTRIGUE **4** : to do something customarily **5** : to take advantage of someone ⟨he *practised* on their credulity with huge success —*Times Lit. Supp.*⟩ — **prac·tic·er** *n*]

TO DEFINE ARCHITECTURE as practice would seem uncontroversial, if not self-evident. It is a straightforward description of what architects do on a day-to-day basis. That is to say, architects practice architecture in the same sense that doctors practice medicine or attorneys practice law. Yet ambitious architects everywhere seem inclined to define what they do as something other than the simple exercise of professional practice. "Inquiry," "interrogation," "critique," or "investigation," and "poetics," "discourse," "information design," or "research" are some of the code words for practice today. Refusing the simple pleasures of professional know-how, architects seem to prefer the reflected prestige of science or art.

Why this skepticism toward a simple definition of professional expertise? If we define practice as the informed application of professional knowledge, usually in return for commercial gain, or as the habitual exercise of a profession and the acquisition of proficiency through repetition, it would seem that two objections might arise. The first is the delimited nature of professional expertise, suggesting as it does a closed, or rote, kind of knowledge. The second is the taint of commercialism.

Now Stephen Cassell and Adam Yarinsky, the principals of ARO, understand very well that in any profession there are those who operate by rote, at minimal professional standards, and there are those capable of imagination, invention, and creative thinking, in short, those working to push the limits of the discipline. Professional expertise is the starting point for the work of ARO, but it is only a starting point, a foothold to begin a much more complicated process of research, design, and execution. Likewise, they do not shy away from the entrepreneurial aspect of architecture. A successful commercial practice has put them in contact with clients capable of supporting their ongoing design research, and it allows them to maintain the office infrastructure necessary to practice on their own terms. For ARO, it has always been more important to be good than to be different; yet they also show that by being good, they stand out as different.

Quite apart from the compelling results of this partnership, I would argue that a large part of ARO's contribution has been to revive the notion of practice as the central intellectual activity of the architect. In other words, their practice is not the reflection or illustration of ideas articulated elsewhere; it is itself an ongoing source of ideas. Their experiments with materials and fabrication, their collaborations with innovative consultants, and their open design process are as much an exercise of the mind as of the hand. Their example affirms that it is possible to produce architectural concepts by means of the materials and procedures of architecture itself, without recourse to language or concepts borrowed from other fields.

Two career models are present in architecture today. The first, and older model, proposes an incremental increase in scale and complexity. For the generation of the New York Five, for example, the typical pattern was to begin with small-scale residential works and to move gradually up in scale to civic or institutional commissions. More recently, another career model has emerged, associated with the generation (if not the personalities) of Rem Koolhaas, Zaha Hadid, or Bernard Tschumi. Here, a young architect rises to a level of high visibility through publications, conferences, and gallery exhibitions, and moves directly on to building at a larger scale through competitions or institutionally sanctioned commissions.

ARO belongs to yet another generation, and the firm frustrates the expectations of both models. From the beginning ARO took on projects of a high degree of complexity, and they continue to work simultaneously at large and small scales. Moreover, operating as they do under the rules of a new information-driven economy, logistical complexity is no longer directly linked to scale. Some of ARO's relatively small commissions have budgets and scale more often associated with institutional projects. Like many of their contemporaries, ARO's partners understand that the opportunities for architectural practice today are at once more restrictive and more open: more restrictive in the sense that there are many talented people competing for a small pool of work; yet more open in that the fluidity of the new economy creates opportunities in unexpected places. If you are willing to define architectural practice broadly, and to take on unconventional challenges, new possibilities open up. ARO's flexibility has been rewarded with a wide variety of projects in both the public and private realm.

Although both partners have taught and are comfortable in the academic world, they have never let themselves get too comfortable. Teaching has always been secondary to practice for ARO; for them, practice is not, as is the case with many young architects, a subsidized sideline to a teaching career. They have built their practice through practice, creating a network of clients, collaborators, and consultants that in turn allows them to continually refine their practice. That they have managed to support themselves and their office without compromising the quality of their work is no small accomplishment. There are no backroom, "bread-and-butter" projects in this office.

So what then are the defining characteristics of this practice? It is first, as might be expected, "research"-driven, but I think there is some potential for confusion here. For ARO, research is not disinterested academic inquiry; it is not the reinterpretation, or critique, of existing material. In other words, it is not oriented toward the past, but is instead forward-looking. It is applied research, "investigation or experimentation" directed at the "revision of accepted theories" and the "practical application of such new or revised theories." Research is a product, motivated by the demands of specific commissions. ARO uses research instrumentally, to find new ways of doing things: alternative materials and means of fabrication, or unexpected solutions to newly emerging design problems. It is a collaborative process, based on the open exchange of ideas among the partners, staff, and consultants. It manifests an intellectual curiosity. Solutions are never repeated; rather, each new problem is studied for its own particular challenges and potentials. In many cases, the answer to a given problem is not a formal solution, but a new way of approaching the problem itself. Complexity, in the work of ARO, is present in materials, details, and procedures of realization, but never as an arbitrary formal complexity. Their work is hands-on and material-specific, and respects the expertise of consultants and collaborators in other fields. It has a strong connection to contemporary urban culture. ARO has designed private domestic spaces in the city, as well as places of consumption and publicity. While these are not the conventional sites of the urban public realm, more and more they are becoming the primary places of contemporary urban experience. Finally, Stephen Cassell and Adam Yarinsky are committed modernists. This is not to suggest that they approach architecture from an ideological or stylistic point of view, but rather that the principles of modern architecture serve as a starting point for their ongoing work process. In the diverse experiences of modernism, ARO finds an open catalogue of solutions appropriate to contemporary construction technology and to modern lifestyles.

Nearly any of ARO's projects could exemplify these characteristics, but perhaps the one that best makes the case is the US Armed Forces Recruiting Station in Times Square. The general issues of the project are clear. It can be seen as an intelligent reworking of Robert Venturi's notion of the decorated shed and as an almost inevitable response to a highly loaded context. Given the political content of the program, the architects have withheld judgment, proposing instead a building that declares in a very direct way what it is and conceals nothing of what goes on inside. Yet two aspects of ARO's response stand out. Of course, the idea of the building as sign is nothing new. But here, the sign is not an opaque appliqué over a neutral structure, but is instead integral to the transparent facade membrane itself. Sign, structure, and enclosure form a continuous whole. Moreover, by coupling semiotic information, which could be seen as the primary trope of postmodernism, with transparency, one of the signature tropes of modernism, ARO created a strange and unstable mixture, which is in large part responsible for the power of this small building. This random sampling of available strategies, without regard for their origin, exemplifies ARO's postideological pragmatism. What works in the field is more important than the idea's intellectual provenance. A telling detail is the camouflage coloring painted on the roof. The patterned roof not only recognizes that this is a building seen as often from above as from the street, but also hints at the architects' more general reading of the site and program. Resting lightly on an existing subway grating, the building has something of the feel of a provisional structure, or a temporary occupation of the site. As a simple matter of tactics, ARO understood that in this noisy environment, a modest structure can actually have a greater presence by being less assertive. That is to say, the building's uncanny ability to disappear into the context at certain times means that when it does appear, it is with renewed force.

But if it is true that in large measure the innovations of ARO are more at the level of process than form, then the logistical challenges of realizing this building need to be mentioned. There is a very important diagram included in the documentation of the recruiting station. This chart details a demanding process of political review that included, beyond the usual regulating agencies, a cast of characters that ranged from the Department of Defense to the New York City Transit Authority, to Nancy Sinatra, the New York City Arts Commission, and the Mayor's Office of Veterans' Affairs. To be able to shepherd a project through this maze of approvals, and to be able to satisfy such a diverse constituency without losing sight of the fundamental quality of the design itself, shows remarkable tenacity and resourcefulness. Under this kind of scenario (more often associated with large-scale institutional work) it becomes more important than ever that the architectural concepts be strong and simple. The architecture needs to speak clearly to a diverse audience and cannot depend on obscure arguments. A well-defined role for architectural expertise— that is to say, the power of strong design concepts and precise technical knowledge— allowed ARO to function effectively throughout this complex process.

Taken together, the defining characteristics of the recruiting station—formal sophistication; clarity of architectural logic; innovative, materially specific technical solutions; and a robust yet flexible strategy of implementation—are also the more general reference points for ARO's practice. They outline a strategy for making refined and lasting works of architecture, works that will not fade away with shifting fashions. They cut across scale and program, and therefore position the firm well for the challenges to come.

Philip Johnson has famously remarked that for an architect life begins at fifty. Somewhat more obliquely, Rem Koolhaas has defined the typology of the successful career in architecture as one in which up to age fifty-five, you can do anything you want, but no one will give you work; after that, you get more work than you can handle, but have nothing left to say. ARO has already proven these icons wrong, and I am confident that they will continue to confound these reasonable expectations.

1. *Merriam-Webster's Collegiate Dictionary* (Springfield, MA: Merriam-Webster, Incorporated), 2002.

THE EAST AND WEST FACADES of the US Armed Forces Recruiting Station display two large illuminated American flags. This design is both a response to the project's extraordinary site as well as part of a strategy for designing and building the station in a very short time and through a complex review process. The singular gesture of the flag was intended to be easily

ing replaces an existing 1950s recruiting station and is restricted to the same site, footprint, and height limitations. It sits on top of an existing subway ventilation grill within a narrow triangular traffic median. The building houses a modest program: four desks (one for each branch of the military) and a bathroom. On this limited site, the building is dwarfed by

US Armed Forces Recruiting Station, TIMES SQUARE, NEW YORK, NEW YORK

understood and quickly approved. Yet, in the context of Times Square, this simple idea obtains a more complex meaning. Through the reflections of its environment, the flag is integrated with the surrounding signage of Times Square, fluctuating between an unequivocal patriotic symbol and a commercial advertisement. Through these multiple perceptions of the building, the project proposes a new interpretation of public architecture.

Drawn by the visibility and activity of Times Square, one of the busiest urban areas in the world, the military first located a temporary recruiting structure on the site during World War II. The new 520-square-foot build-

the enormous size of its surrounding context.

To maximize its impact, every aspect of the design is meant to reinforce the reading of the flag, which is made of fluorescent light fixtures located between the building's structural columns and glass facades. A staggered pattern of fixtures is used for the stripes, while the stars have a stacked pattern. The light bulbs are covered with translucent reflective colored gels to make the red, white, and blue colors visible both at night and during the day. Echoing the movement of Broadway and Seventh Avenue, the different spacings of the structure, lighting, and mullions create the illusion that they are slipping relative to each other,

architecture research office

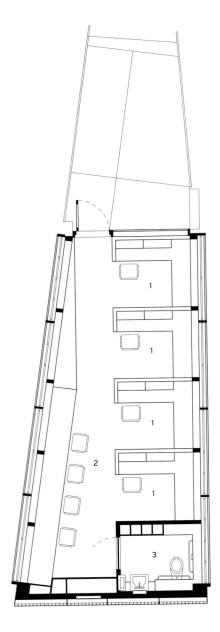

0'   5'

1 Desk
2 Testing area
3 Bathroom

making the flag appear to float distinct from the enclosing walls.

The materials and details for the station were selected and developed to reinforce the primary design idea. Clad in louvered aluminum panels, the south elevation forms a neutral, shadowy field upon which the signage for each military branch sits. Behind these panels are risers for power and water, a ladder to the roof, and an access door for controlling the illuminated ball that is dropped on New Year's Eve. Stainless steel, chosen for its durability and moderately reflective quality, is used for the building's cladding and for the window mullions. The cross section of the structure allows roof access and eliminates the need for a distracting handrail. Inside, this section is registered in a curvilinear dropped ceiling, which mediates between the large scale of the exterior

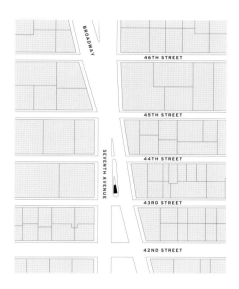

and the small scale of the interior, creating a white surface against which the flag is seen from outside. Gray rubber flooring, stainless steel countertops, and maple workstation partitions are the interior materials. Visible from all of the surrounding skyscrapers, the roof is painted an urban camouflage pattern of gray, black, and white.

Diagram of reviewing agencies

Senator "X" **1**

US Department of Defense (commissioning agency) **2**

Joint Recruiting Forces Committee client (reviewing agency) **3**

US Army Corps of Engineers (implementing agency)

USACE Northeast Division (assigning agency)

USACE New York District (implementing client rep.)

USACE NY District Engineering Office (reviewing client rep. through CDs)

USACE NY District Project Management Office **4**

Parsons Brinckerhoff (our client and engineer)

Construction Inc. (contractor) **5**

ARO

Department of Transportation

Chief Engineer

Borough Engineer

Highway Office

Pedestrian Mobility Office

OCMC

Permits

Nancy Sinatra **6**

Mayor's Office of Veterans' Affairs **7**

Department of Buildings

Manhattan Borough President

Community Board 5

Flag-in-Plexiglas-Box Lady **8**

New York City Arts Commission

Mayor's Office for People with Disabilities

NY Transit Authority (state agency) **9**

Times Square Business Improvement District

USACE NY District Construction Office

USACE Metro Area Construction Office (CM) client rep. through CA

1 The building was originally scheduled to be finished by the Fourth of July. To mark the completion of the project, a general wanted to have an elaborate celebration, including a jet flyover. However, the start of construction was delayed until mid-May. Although it was clear that the July Fourth deadline could not be met, no one at the US Army Corps of Engineers wanted to inform the general. Therefore, the contractor was instructed to speed up the work. As a consequence, construction quality slipped to an unacceptable level. The distinguished senator from New York, an architecture buff, was contacted. The senator chaired the Senate Appropriations Committee, which controlled the US Army Corps of Engineers' budget. Within twenty-four hours the project's schedule was extended, and faulty work was removed and replaced.

2 The recruiting station contains four desks, one for each branch of the military. The purpose, history, and culture of each branch is completely different. This is manifest in distinct seals, symbols, and color schemes. The American flag was one symbol that every branch could agree upon.

3 The project was presented to the Joint Recruiting Forces Committee, which consisted of representatives of the Pentagon and the different services. The members of the committee fired questions throughout the presentation. At the end of the presentation, an Air Force colonel joked that if the project was over budget, the architect and engineer would be shot.

4 ARO and Parsons Brinckerhoff were given three months to complete the design, construction drawing, and approvals process. During these three months ARO and Parsons Brinckerhoff had forty meetings with the different parties listed on the diagram. The first day of the project, the project manager for the US Army Corps of Engineers advised ARO to "not make it too good and not make it too bad, just slide it on through."

5 The contractor for the project was selected through a government low-bid process. The US Army Corps of Engineers was unaware that the same contractor (with a different company name) was being sued by a different division of the Corps. The contractor obtained permission from the Corps to rent valuable space on the construction fence to advertisers for more money than the daily penalty levied by the client for a late project.

6 Frank Sinatra died while the project was under construction. Nancy Sinatra offered to donate a larger-than-life statue of her father to the city. (The statue included a speaker that continuously played Frank Sinatra songs.) She wanted the statue to sit in front of the recruiting station, which is located across the street from the site of the Paramount Theater, where Frank Sinatra performed. The site plan of the island was reworked to accommodate the statue. The statue was never installed.

7 The local assemblyman opposed replacing the existing station due to the treatment of gays in the military. Mayor Giuliani offered to back the project. He required that the station be designed and built very quickly before anyone could mount serious opposition to it. To help expedite the process, he had the head of the Mayor's Office of Veterans' Affairs shepherd the project through the approval process.

8 For many years the previous recruiting station on the site had a tattered flag, as there was no access to the roof of the structure to remove it. One woman, who was offended by the condition of the flag, proposed housing it in a protective Plexiglas box that would attach to the top of the flagpole. She was well known to numerous officials for championing this idea at every opportunity.

9 The station sits on top of a subway grate that is under the jurisdiction of the NY Transit Authority. The NY Transit Authority's approval time frame was longer than the project's overall design and construction schedule. In order to shorten the review process, it was necessary to demonstrate that the project would have no impact on the Transit Authority. Therefore, the building was designed to be dragged forward off of the subway grate, in case the space below the building needed to be reached.

17

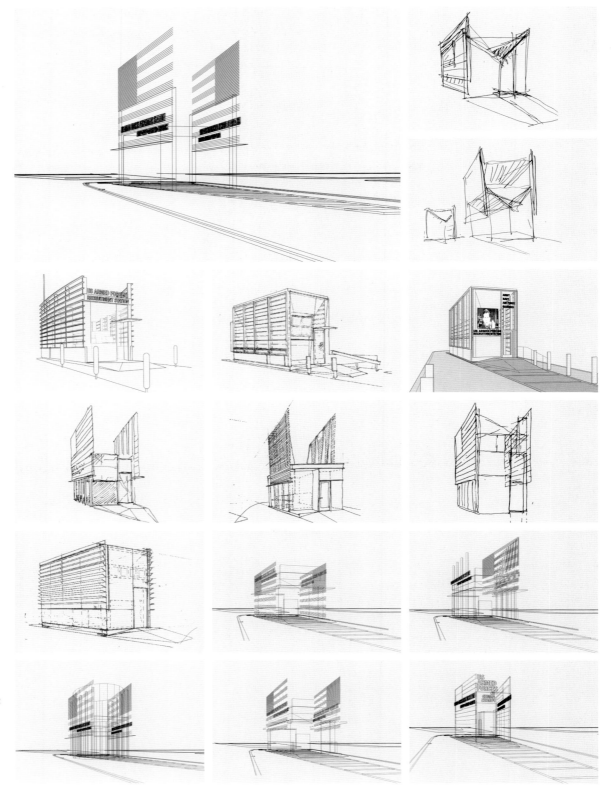

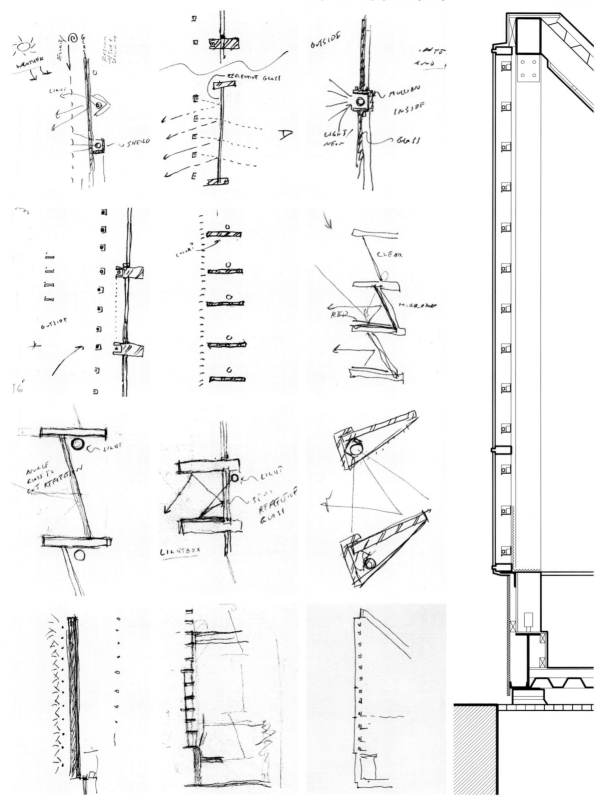

Lighting layout of flag elevation

L1/BLUE	L1/BLUE	L1/BLUE	L1/BLUE	L1/BLUE	L1/BLUE	L1/BLUE	L1/RED
L1/BLUE	L1/BLUE	L1/BLUE	L1/BLUE	L1/BLUE	L1/BLUE	L1/BLUE	L1/WHITE
L1/BLUE	L1/BLUE	L1/BLUE	L1/BLUE	L1/BLUE	L1/BLUE	L1/BLUE	L1/RED
L1/BLUE	L1/BLUE	L1/BLUE	L1/BLUE	L1/BLUE	L1/BLUE	L1/BLUE	L1/WHITE
L1/BLUE	L1/BLUE	L1/BLUE	L1/BLUE	L1/BLUE	L1/BLUE	L1/BLUE	L1/RED
L1/BLUE	L1/BLUE	L1/BLUE	L1/BLUE	L1/BLUE	L1/BLUE	L1/BLUE	L1/WHITE
L1/BLUE	L1/BLUE	L1/BLUE	L1/BLUE	L1/BLUE	L1/BLUE	L1/BLUE	L1/RED

L1/WHITE	L2/WHITE		L1/WHITE	L1/WHITE	L2/WHITE		L1/WHITE

L2/RED	L2/RED	L2/RED	L2/RED

L1/WHITE	L2/WHITE		L1/WHITE	L1/WHITE	L2/WHITE		L1/WHITE

L2/RED	L2/RED	L2/RED	L2/RED

L1/WHITE	L2/WHITE		L1/WHITE	L1/WHITE	L2/WHITE		L1/WHITE

L2/RED	L2/RED	L2/RED	L2/RED

architecture research office

2/RED   L2/RED   L2/RED   L2/RED

1/WHITE   L2/WHITE   L1/WHITE   L1/WHITE   L2/WHITE   L1/WHITE

2/RED   L2/RED   L2/RED   L2/RED

/WHITE   L2/WHITE   L1/WHITE   L1/WHITE   L2/WHITE   L1/WHITE

2/RED   L2/RED   L2/RED   L2/RED

/WHITE   L2/WHITE   L1/WHITE   L1/WHITE   L2/WHITE   L1/WHITE

2/RED   L2/RED   L2/RED   L2/RED

/WHITE   L2/WHITE   L1/WHITE   L1/WHITE   L2/WHITE   L1/WHITE

/RED   L2/RED   L2/RED   L2/RED

WHITE   L2/WHITE   L1/WHITE   L1/WHITE   L2/WHITE   L1/WHITE

/RED   L2/RED   L2/RED   L2/RED

WHITE   L2/WHITE   L1/WHITE   L1/WHITE   L2/WHITE   L1/WHITE

/RED   L2/RED   L2/RED   L2/RED

THE INTEGRATION OF COMPUTER REPRESENTATION in architecture and design, and the fabrication capabilities of computer-controlled equipment allow for a direct connection between the architect/designer and the finished product, changing the relationship between thinking and making. Computer-Aided Design/Computer-Aided Manufacture (CAD/CAM) has the potential to transtwo-dimensional uses (the laser cutter operates on flat materials) rather than starting with three-dimensional applications. Initial studies were made with a standardized test pattern on three-by-five-inch pieces of different materials and consisted of methodically changing one of the laser's three settings: speed, power, and pulses per inch. As an intuitive familiarity with

Paper Wall, Artists Space, NEW YORK, NEW YORK

form the making of architecture in ways that are both fundamental and beautiful as it creates new material possibilities and gives the designer an unprecedented level of participation in the construction process.

ARO's research for the paper wall began as an exploration of two separate but related areas; the first was to learn how a computer-controlled laser cutter could be used as a design tool, and the second, to explore how the capabilities of the laser cutter and the properties of a specific medium (paper) could inform an installation at Artists Space gallery in SoHo, New York City. CAD/CAM technology was engaged at a basic level by considering the laser cutter's simplest possible

the laser cutter developed, many more variables were considered, including the chronology of the laser cuts and the force of the air that ventilates the machine over the material. This knowledge informed the process of designing and making.

Simultaneously, a series of studies examined the physical characteristics of paper, and how a single paper unit could be fabricated, tiled (to create a continuous surface), and formed into a three-dimensional shape. The material properties of paper, including its ability to bend, fold, twist, crumple, and tear, acquired a new dimension through the laser cutter. Paper's tensile and compressive properties, its connective abilities, and volumetric potential were explored.

architecture research office

In the process, paper was transformed as new textures and translucency were achieved.

For the Artists Space gallery, ARO designed and fabricated a freestanding paper wall using laser-cut and manually folded units that were joined with minimal mechanical fastening. The size of each unit was dictated by the maximum eighteen-by-twenty-four-inch cutting area of the laser cutter. Several test walls, each based upon a different unit design and structural strategy, were built to develop the form and construction of the installation. Each unit's shape, texture, and color, and the connections between units, were informed by the initial explorations of laser-cut paper. The final wall consisted of stacked interlocking opaque and translucent units, each of which had a flat exterior surface and a bowed interior, finely striated with alternating cuts removed. The strawlike result was then interwoven with adjacent units, allowing the units to shift and reposition themselves as subsequent rows were added in a running-bond pattern. The inner core of the wall was illuminated to accentuate the depth and texture of the entire assembly.

The project was a success, although the wall collapsed on the night of the exhibition opening. Unforeseen field conditions, including an uneven floor and the close proximity of a large crowd of people, compromised the fragile structural balance of the wall. However, the research from this project is ongoing, and knowledge gained from this exploration has influenced other work in the office.

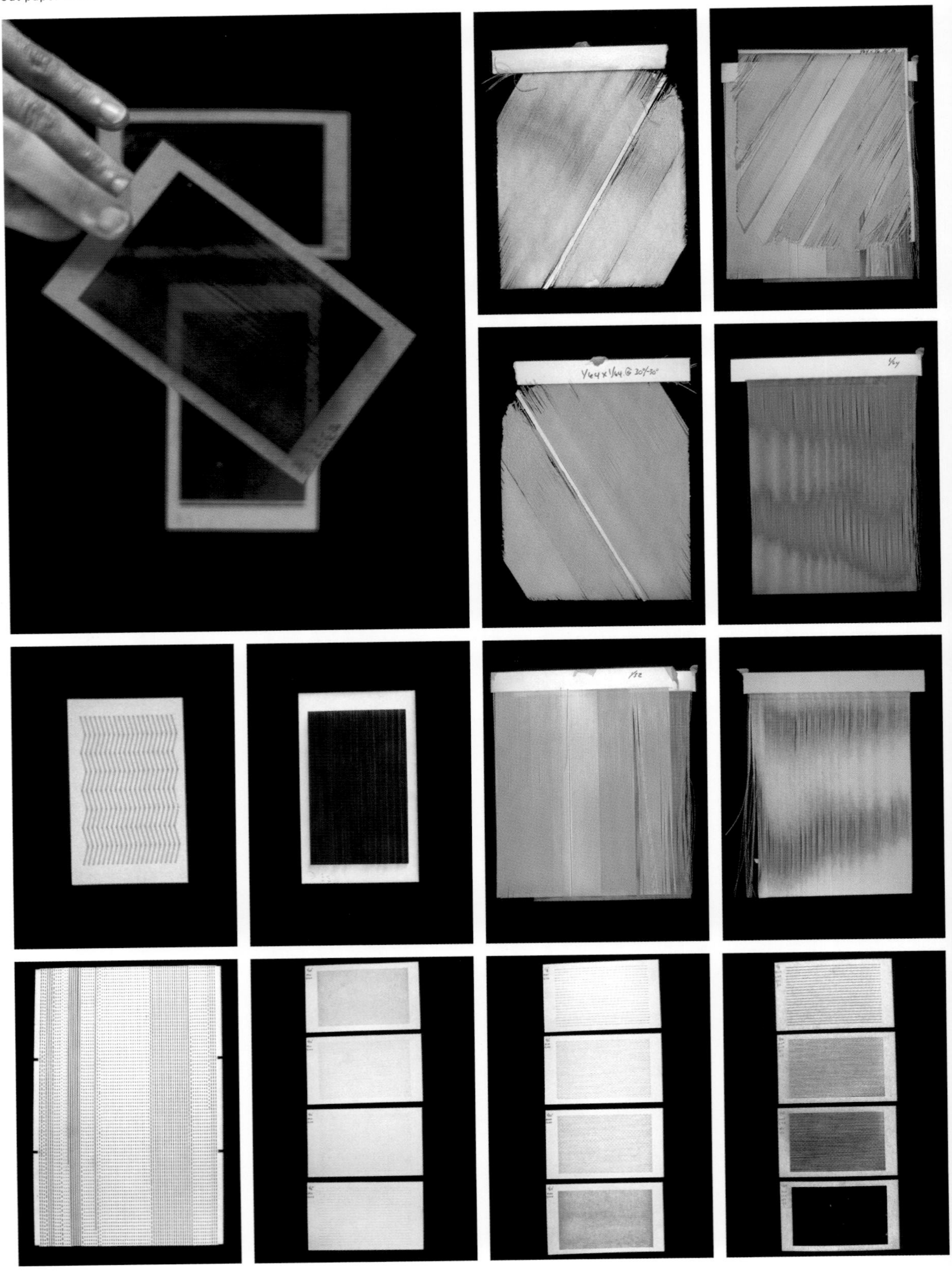

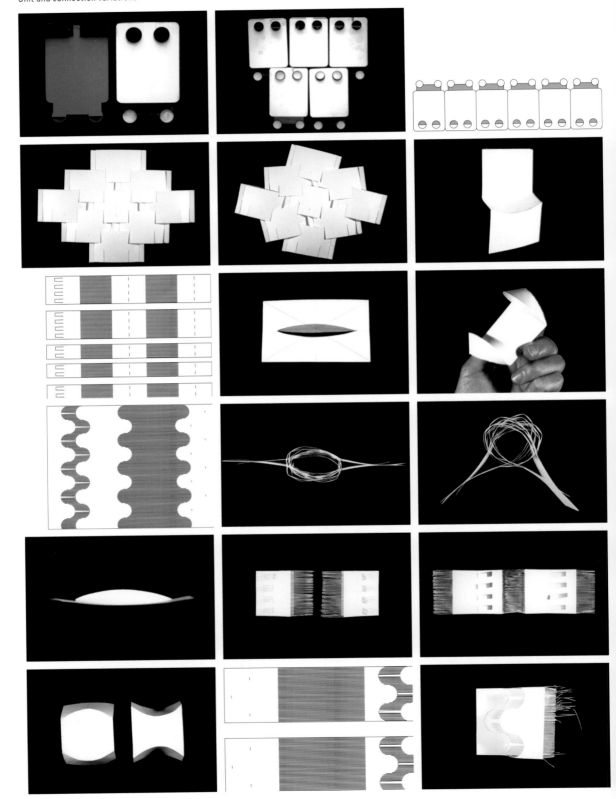

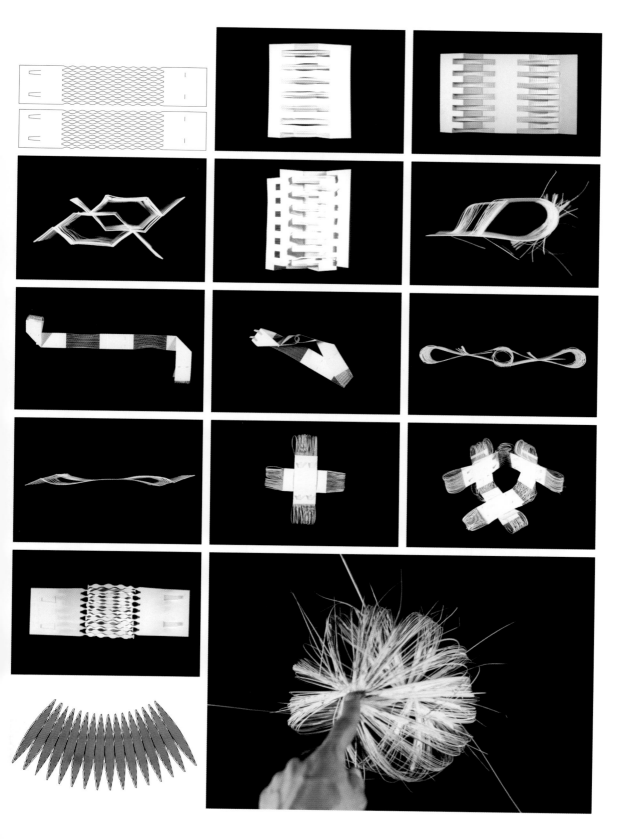

39

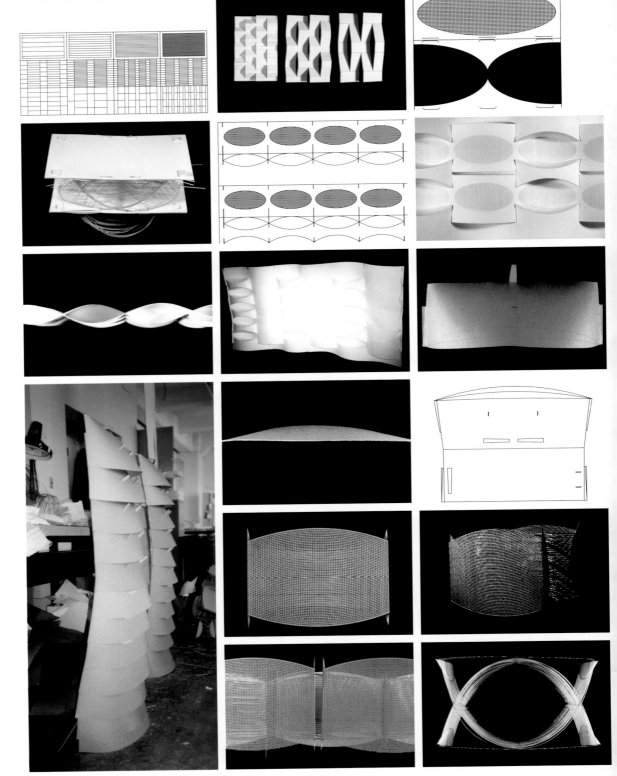

two units from one eighteen-by-twenty-four-inch sheet of bristol board

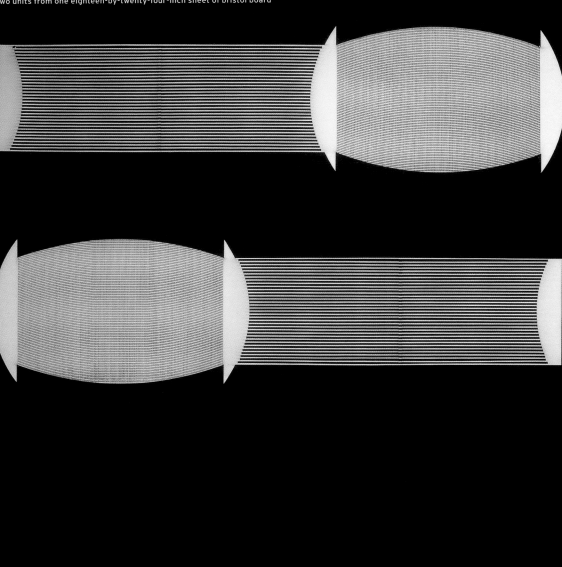

architecture research office

Chart of varying unit types

	half unit	standard unit	bottom unit	lintel
opaque unit variations				
opaque unit with hook				
final opaque unit				
low-density hatch unit				
high-density hatch unit				

Final installation of paper wall in the gallery

architecture research office

Collapsed wall at the exhibition opening

Facts Plus

Sarah Whiting

IN 1947 HENRY-RUSSELL HITCHCOCK cleanly separated the world of architectural practice into two camps: the bureaucrats and the geniuses.[1] In 1956 Colin Rowe shifted the division to Americans versus Europeans. Understanding Rowe's argument in Hitchcock's terms is easy, especially when Rowe writes that "In Chicago it might be said that the frame was convincing as fact rather than as idea, whereas in considering the European innovators of the twenties one cannot suppress the supposition that the frame to them was much more often an essential idea before it was an altogether reasonable fact."[2] Burnham was a *bureaucrat* and Mies was a *genius*: "the Chicago architects had 'frankly accepted the conditions imposed by the speculator'—they had limited themselves to producing buildings which should be no more than the logical instruments of investment," whereas the Europeans saw the frame as "the answer to the universal problem, architecture."[3]

ARO's architectural genius lies in their exploitation of this decidedly American lineage: the architecture of convincing facts. While the world of facts was for the Chicago School a "pragmatic and rational" path that resulted in an architecture that was, according to Rowe, "paradigmatic and normative," ARO operates in a universe that is at once factual and sensual, researched and liberating, singular and multiple. Theirs is an architecture of effervescent pragmatism.

Rather than bemoan a (perhaps too facile) characterization of American architecture as lacking enlightened clients, public monies, and more flexible relations with the building industry (conditions often ascribed to our European counterparts), ARO has established a practice that thrives on its heritage of a carefully subjugated Protestantism. This is to say that it emerges from an American academic lineage—a lineage of *work as idea*—to pursue an architecture that supersedes its own facts. The firm has developed an "Americanism" of highly specific choice: an Americanism that is not that of Colin Rowe's *clear ambiguity*, nor that of Robert Venturi's messy vitality. Rather, it is a *clean multiplicity* that evolves from both.

ARO's clean multiplicity is an architecture that is deliberately researched, rigorously defined, and consciously constructed but that nevertheless continually opens itself to multiple interpretations, audiences, and subjectivities. To achieve this particular combination of specificity and variety, ARO combines Rowe's formal politics with Venturi's rhetorical contextualism, but alters both by combining them with a dose of contemporary research into materials and their effects.

Adam Yarinsky and Stephen Cassell are heirs to Colin Rowe's legacy of mid-twentieth-century liberalism, a politics already described by Alexis de Tocqueville early in the nineteenth century as a continuous exchange between the individual and a collective. This politics is not that of a May '68 oppositional critique, nor is it a normative politics that mutely accepts the status quo; instead, it subscribes to the liberal embrace of tenuous coherency. It is a system built upon a ubiquitous, if fragile, communicability across the vast differentials that permeate contemporary life. This commonality requires a certain architectural legibility that is based upon shared cultural languages—visual as well as verbal. For Rowe, the rules of this shared code emanated from precedent and other legal methodologies that established the very culture of architecture.[4]

Rowe's architectural language relied upon the visual recognition of historical precedents and their transformations. ARO's shared language similarly originates in the visual, but unlike Rowe's historically discursive liberalism, theirs is a material liberalism, which generates multiple sensory repercussions. Their projects foster public collectives while simultaneously maintaining individualities, as in the Qiora Store and Spa in New York, which embeds the very personal and highly individualized experience of getting a massage directly within the midst of a retail space. The formal ambiguity of the spaces within Qiora is amplified by the softness of the lighting and the materials—organza fabric panels offer layers of translucency and create tentative associations among the discretely dispersed shoppers. Rather than designing a space of radical disorientation, or normative definition, ARO envisioned Qiora as a space of possible associations, among people, environments (simultaneously aqueous, aerial, futurist, meditative, and scientific), and programs. Like Rowe, ARO relies upon precedents, but these precedents are no longer limited to the academic pantheon of architectural history. Qiora offers a perfect illustration of what Cassell calls *simultaneity*: "the specific economic and social and material context of each project in the real world...[It is] about coming up with a solution that does not have a specific language but that's generated out of the space and the context of each problem."[5]

In 1950 Robert Venturi had a "Eureka!" moment when he recognized the possibilities that Gestalt psychology's analysis of our perceptual context might offer architecture. This revelation became the root of his M.F.A. design thesis at Princeton that year. Focusing on context (a topic shunned by the period's modernist proclivities), Venturi explained that "its implication for the designer is that existing conditions around the site that should become a part of any design problem should be respected, and that through the designer's control of the relation of the old and new he can perceptually enhance the existing by means of the new."[6] With this thesis, Venturi transformed modernism, jettisoning autonomy in favor of contextualism. While architects today are in turn shunning contextualism in an attempt to distance themselves from the rampant two-dimensional contextual semiotics that dominated postmodern historicism, ARO has embraced Venturi's legacy of engaging context. Like Venturi, ARO deploys contextualism in the name of a kind of populist legibility; but for them, legibility readily harvests materiality, landscape, and multiple sensory readings of a project, in addition to the simple visual legibility of "signs."

The US Armed Forces Recruiting Station at Times Square in Manhattan—undeniably ARO's most Venturi-like project—is a glass box that traffics in the transparent functionalism of mid-century modernism (echoing the radical transparency of SOM's Manufacturers Hanover Trust bank building of 1954, for example) and in the rhetoric of an occupiable symbol, an enormous American flag whose fluorescent tubes reflect the neon urbanism of 42nd Street. As Yarinsky notes, "the building appears both reflective and transparent, depending on ambient lighting conditions and the position of the viewer."[7] In other words, the viewers of the structure are at once unified (all who see the building "read" the flag, for instance) and separate (any singular apprehension of the structure is compounded by multiplicitous readings that are embodied in its ever-changing reflections and transparencies as one moves around the building).

Yarinsky and Cassell's insistence upon creating collectives while maintaining individualities appears in several other ARO projects. While most do so within the public realm, the Colorado House accomplishes this overlap of collective and individual at the domestic scale, offering "large spaces for family gatherings" as well as "intimate areas for personal contemplation."[8] While these two kinds of spaces are the result of ARO's manipulations of scale, furnishings, and organization in the plan of the house, they are rendered legible primarily through their relation to the landscape. The spaces for large gatherings have the dramatic mountain landscape as their primary panorama backdrop, whereas the more intimate spaces obtain these panoramas while nestling within the proximate landscape—a bedroom protrudes gently into an aspen grove, for example.

In the Columbia War Remembrance Memorial project, ARO's strategy of edited contextualism is used toward a similar end. Here, materiality is the primary vehicle for achieving this goal. The physical elements of the campus's public spaces (shrubs, brick, granite, bronze) are combined to make a whole—a fifty-by-thirty-foot occupiable memorial shrub containing walls—that permits variations in its interpretation (each war is demarcated with its own bronze wall; each individual who died is singled out by a facet on those walls). The experience of the memorial is at once informal and structured—highly individualized as an experience, but codified as a formal, collective encounter. Through its sensory and material relationships, the memorial's architectural contextualism extends beyond the primacy of visual perception that dominated the lineage inherited from Rowe and Venturi.

Despite their perceptual biases, all of these projects sit firmly within the "factual" realm; none—not even the US Armed Forces Recruiting Station—offer an ideological agenda. But while facts suggest a one-to-one relationship between cause and effect—repeatable, predictable, normative—ARO's "facts plus" generate unforeseen possibilities. Perhaps the most idea-saturated factual investigation conducted by ARO is their paper wall, which resulted from research into computer-aided design manufacturing technologies. Paying no heed to the story of the three little pigs, the project hovers between the absurd and the pragmatic, constructing a wall out of a material that is in itself extraordinarily unstructured but is readily available: paper. The project is documented like a scientific experiment of exhaustive iterations, but its result is less pragmatic than utilitarian. It does not try to change the world. It is, simply, beautiful. The optimism and positivism underlying the paper wall and ARO's other projects is undeniably fresh in the vast puddle of cynicism and irony that surrounds us today. The challenge for this young firm will be to further convince us of the potential for facts to become transcendent—for materiality, research, and ultimately architecture to turn facts into ideas.

Thank you to Nicola Bednarek and especially to Ron Witte for their thoughtful suggestions regarding this text.

1. Henry-Russell Hitchcock, "The Architecture of Bureaucracy and the Architecture of Genius," *The Architectural Review* 101 (January 1947): 3–6.

2. Colin Rowe, "Chicago Frame" (1956), in *The Mathematics of the Ideal Villa and Other Essays* (Cambridge, MA: MIT Press, 1985), 99–101.

3. Ibid., 102, 107.

4. As R. E. Somol explains, "What is crucial for Rowe is the ability for forms to relate isomorphically to a liberal community where discussion (and at least a consensus on procedures if not ends) is possible, against the extremes of both aristocratic idiolects and socialist inevitabilities. This required a vision of an architectural language that was not exhausted by the peculiarities or contingencies of its time, but could allow one, for example, to relate Michelangelo's Villa Farnese to I. M. Pei's Mile High Center in Denver, to concern oneself 'neither with function nor structure…nor with the social context, technology, economics, or content; but simply with the manifestations which reveal themselves to the eye.'" R. E. Somol, "The Law of the Colon," in *In Form Falls Fiction: Misreading the Avantgarde in Contemporary Architecture* (Ph.D. diss., University of Chicago, 1997), 34.

5. Stephen Cassell, as quoted in Philip Nobel, "ARO Introduction," *A+U*, no. 357 (June 2000): 4.

6. Robert Venturi, "Context in Architectural Composition: M.F.A. Thesis, Princeton University," in *Iconography and Electronics upon a Generic Architecture* (Cambridge, MA: MIT Press, 1996), 335.

7. Cf. US Armed Forces Recruiting Station, project description.

8. See Colorado House, project description.

SITUATED ON A REMOTE MESA with spectacular views of the surrounding mountains, the Colorado House is conceived as a frame for the landscape. Accessible by an eight-mile dirt road, the house is located on a knoll at the edge of a meadow surrounded by aspen trees. It is composed of a series of retaining walls and is oriented toward the views of two distant

Colorado House, TELLURIDE, COLORADO

mountain ranges; these two views are at right angles to each other. Stepping down a knoll, the walls slip between the inside and the outside, weaving the 10,000-square-foot house into the site, as each interior space connects directly to an exterior space. The design thus extends the family's love of the outdoors to the daily life of the interior. With these walls and its simple material palette, the building also becomes a frame for the client's collection of furniture and art.

The design balances the family's desire for both large spaces for family gatherings and intimate areas for personal contemplation of the wilderness. The kitchen is the hub of activity

architecture research office

located in the center of the house, while each bedroom is dispersed to the periphery. The relationship between the bedrooms and the group spaces thus provides privacy while forming at the same time a close proximity between the major programs of the house and each bedroom, helping reduce the perceived size of the large building. Where the walls of the house overlap, stairs connect the different levels, creating a clear formal language for the project. The ceiling is faceted with large diagonal panels that respond to the direction of movement in the house and contrast with the rectilinear geometry of the walls. The bedrooms open to the landscape with large walls of glass, giving each family member a specific and distinct view, which simultaneously encompasses the foreground and the distant panorama.

Through extensive visual analysis and design adjustments the landscape was integrated in the project as an active part of the interior experience of the house. The building is oriented so that the Sneffels mountain range can be seen between parallel walls, along their axis. The Ophir Needles, a prominent rock outcropping to the south, appears through wide window openings in the walls. A third view of nearby Sunshine Mountain was also considered in the design. The south-facing strip windows block the foreground view, accentuating the framing of the Ophir Needles. In contrast, the north-facing windows are larger and extend to the floor, visually connecting the interior spaces with the adjacent aspen forest. Additionally, the cross section of the house was adjusted to enable views over its top, even with five feet of snow on the roof.

The materials, detail, and construction of the house reinforce its connection to the landscape. Exterior walls of Cor-Ten shingles rest on sandblasted concrete foundations. The warm reddish-brown color of the shingles relates to the natural site and to the material quality of old mining structures located in the area. The scale and pattern of the shingles reinforce the monolithic quality of the walls and give them a subtle directionality. At certain points the shingles slip into the house, accentuating the close relationship between inside and outside. In contrast, the kitchen wall slips outside, its white surface catching daylight to brighten an adjacent exterior court. The interior walls are covered in white plaster to provide a uniform surface for the display of art, while the floor is a continuous monolithic surface of smooth polished concrete. The two fireplaces are made of dry-laid stone, and the handrails of bead-blasted stainless steel bar. All other detail and material qualities come from the furniture and art that fill the interior.

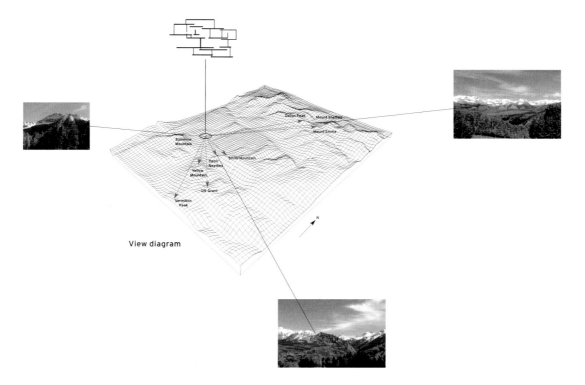

View diagram

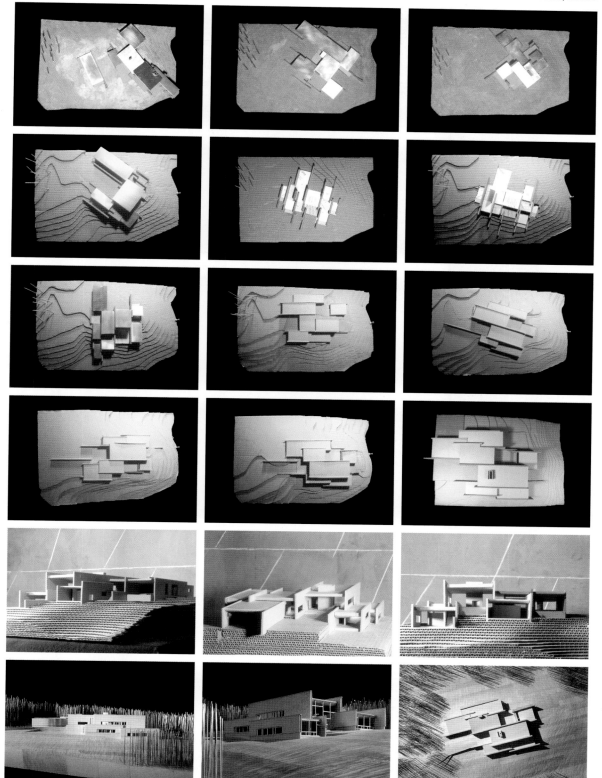

West elevation with the Sneffels mountain range in the distance

architecture research office

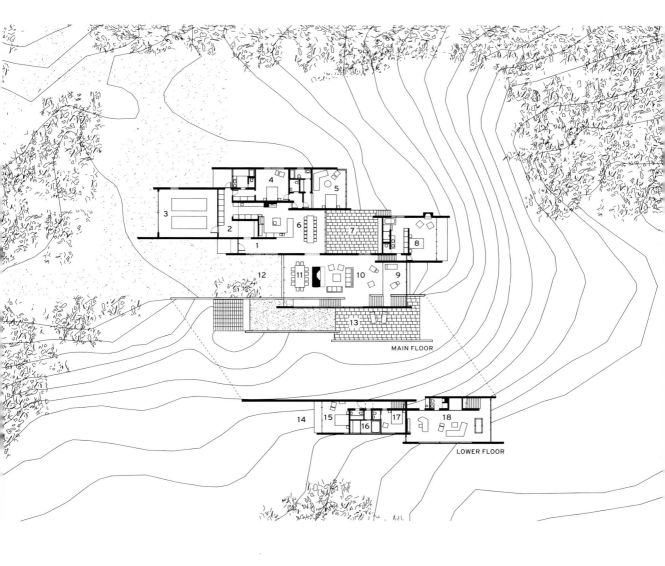

MAIN FLOOR

LOWER FLOOR

Floor plan

1   Entry hall
2   Mud room
3   Garage
4   Guest room
5   Bedroom
6   Kitchen
7   Dining court
8   Master bedroom
9   Sitting room

10   Living room
11   Dining room
12   Sculpture court
13   Ophir Needles terrace
14   Terrace
15   Lower bedroom
16   Steam room
17   Guest room
18   Library/media room

0'   20'

Longitudinal sections

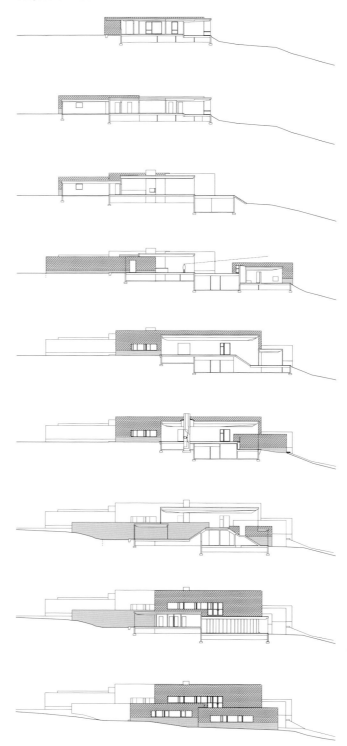

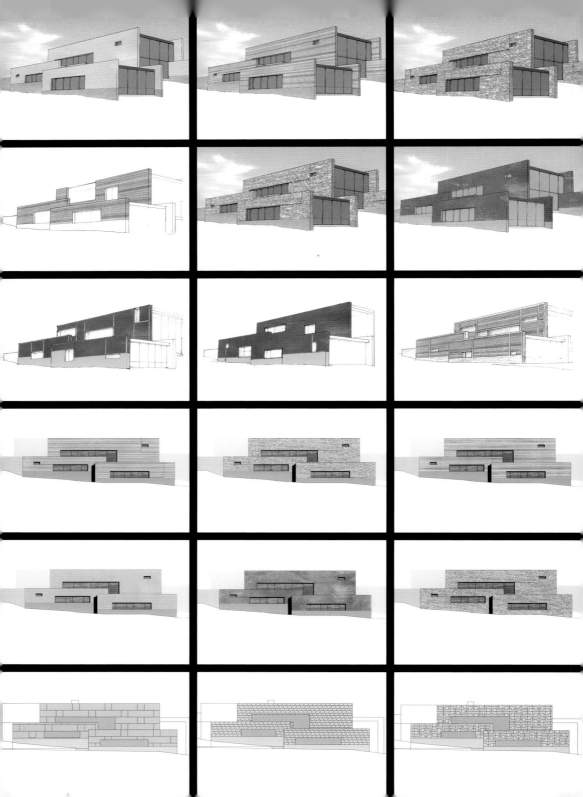

The exterior walls of the house are clad in Cor-Ten steel shingles. The shape of the shingles was chosen so that the pattern can vary depending on the amount of overlap between each row and the orientation of the shingle. The wall assembly is detailed to minimize staining induced by runoff from the Cor-Ten and to eliminate damage to the shingles by removing any water that accumulates behind them. The roughly 10,000 shingles were delivered in special crates designed to allow the shingles to preweather prior to installation.

Entry

architecture research office

Detail of stainless steel shingles in kitchen

architecture research office

Entry hall

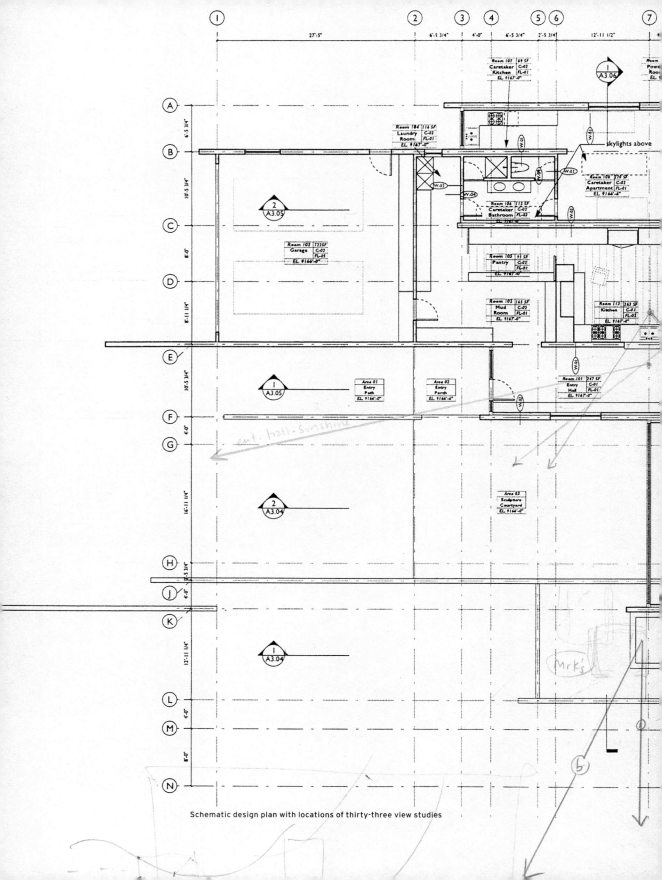

Schematic design plan with locations of thirty-three view studies

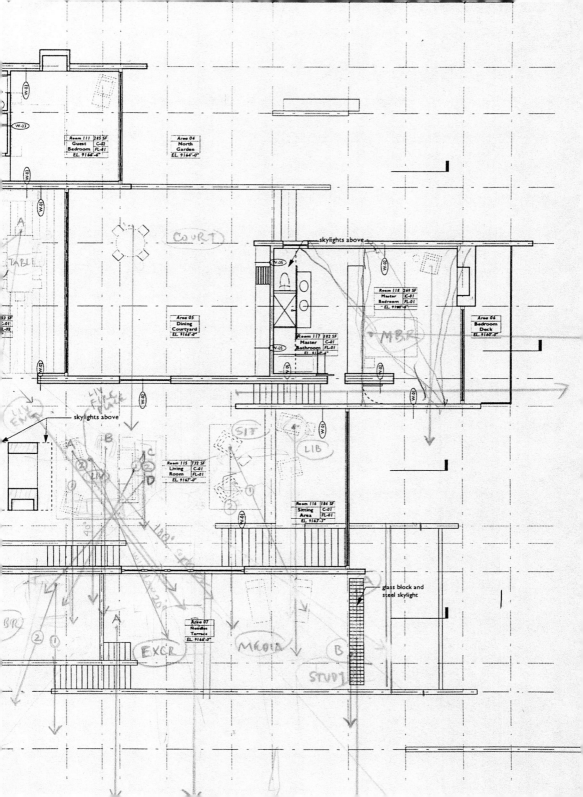

Room 111 265 SF
Guest C-02
Bedroom FL-01
EL 9166'-6"

Area 04
North
Garden
EL 9166'-0"

A

TABLE

COURT

skylights above

W-05

Area 05
Dining
Courtyard
EL 9166'-0"

Room 118 265 SF
Master C-01
Bedroom FL-01
EL 9160'-6"

Area 06
Bedroom
Deck
EL 9160'-6"

Room 117 182 SF
Master C-01
Bathroom FL-01
EL 9160'-6"

M.B.R.

LIV
FIRE
PLACE

LIV
EMT

skylights above

SIT

LIB

A

B

C

LIV

D

Room 115 772 SF
Living C-01
Room FL-01
EL 9167'-0"

Room 116 184 SF
Sitting C-01
Area FL-01
EL 9167'-3"

B/R

glass block and
steel skylight

A

Area 07
Noodles
Terrace
EL 9166'-0"

EXCR

MEDIA

B

STUDY

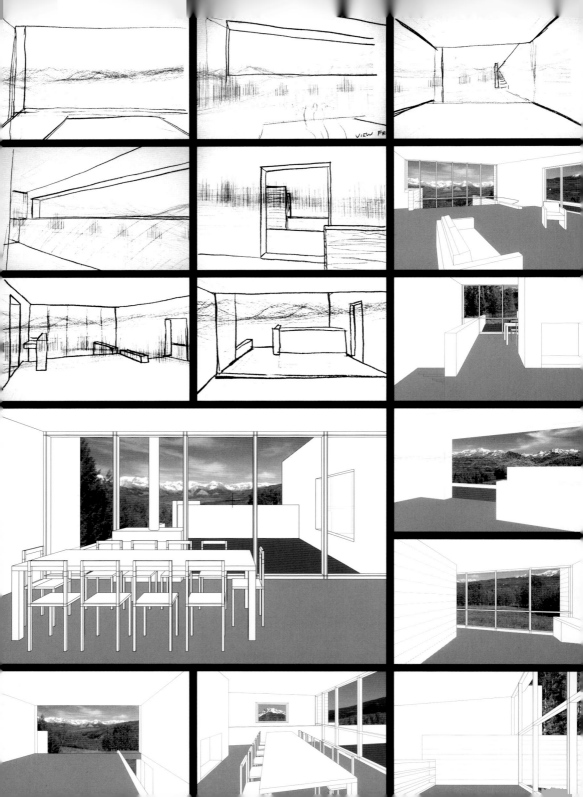

VIEW FR

View from top of lower bedroom stairs

View from bottom of lower bedroom stairs

architecture research office

THIS DESIGN FOR a War Remembrance Memorial at Columbia University was selected on the basis of an invited competition held in 2000. The memorial, which commemorates all Columbia undergraduates who died in combat in wars fought since the founding of the United States, is situated beside a busy pathway within an urban campus. The goal of the project is to recon-

those killed in wars, from prior to 1900 to World War I, World War II, the Korean War, and the Vietnam War. The walls are comprised of cast bronze bricks, each of which is engraved with a name. The length of each wall is thus proportional to the number of students who died in the war that is commemorated. Like the rings of a tree, the position of each wall is located in pro-

War Remembrance Memorial, COLUMBIA UNIVERSITY, NEW YORK, NEW YORK

cile the apparent incongruity of locating a war memorial within Columbia's grounds—the presence of death within the life of the university.

The design proposes a reciprocal relationship with the university in order to weave the memorial into the campus's context. The site of the memorial, adjacent to Low Memorial Library, the central building within the McKim, Mead & White campus plan (designed before the turn of the twentieth century), is a thirty-by-fifty-foot rectangle surrounded by brick-paved walkways. At its center is a mature sycamore tree. In the proposed design, the site is covered with a solid evergreen hedge, which is cut away at five points to include bronze walls that bear the names of

portion to the time that has passed since each war occurred: older wars are closer to the center of the site whereas more recent wars are located toward the edge. Where the walls cut into the hedge, they create areas of contemplation. The canopy of the sycamore tree further defines the space of the memorial.

In order to link it to its surroundings, the memorial is composed of three materials (bronze, hedge, and granite) that are found throughout the campus. Bronze, patinated a greenish-brown, is used in many statues on the university grounds, including Columbia's icon, *Alma Mater*. The walls of the War Remembrance Memorial are made of cast bronze bricks that are stacked in a running

architecture research office

GEORGE EDMOND ALINGH

EWS

ALAN JORDAN BAMI

ARTLETT

MAUF

E

FREDER

WILLIAM JOSEPH CLARK JR

RICK BYRNE

JERRY J. CHERM

GLENN STANLEY DUNBAR

OMBE EHRICHS

EIN

WILLIAM CLANCY EVE

GLENN CHARLES FEINBERG

REDERICKS

LEO MITC

GEORGE HENRY FRITZ

JAMES PARSONS GIFFORD JR.

T GILLESPIE JR.

SIGMUN

CLARENCE ELMORE GITTINS

MELVIN KOBER

KENNETH GORDON LEE

NCIS WILLIAM NEVILLE

bond pattern. The front of each brick gently curves outward to make the name more visible, creating a subtle texture on the wall's surface. This design feature causes the appearance of the walls to change depending on the light conditions. Direct sunlight casts strong shadows that accentuate the individual bricks, whereas indirect ambient light makes the walls appear more monolithic. During the course of the day, the scale of the individual is, through this play of light and shadow, alternately brought forth and subordinated to the entire wall. To modulate the pattern, flat bricks were located intermittently throughout the wall. The evergreen hedge is a species of yew similar to the shrubs that line the edges of the campus's pathways. Planted in a tight grid and clipped in a rectilinear shape, the yew forms a dense mass that helps to define the spaces surrounding each bronze wall. The paving, curbing, and the benches are made of large slabs of Stony Creek granite, a hard stone with a warm red color that is also used elsewhere on the grounds.

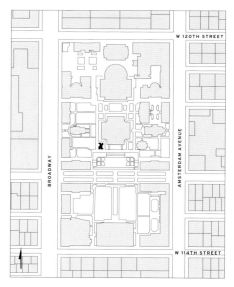

Site plan

architecture research office

Plan studies

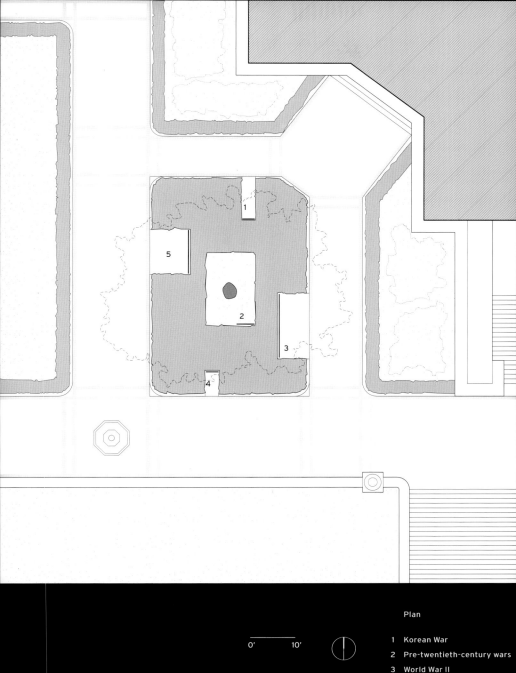

Plan

1   Korean War

2   Pre-twentieth-century wars

3   World War II

0'   10'

WORLD WAR II

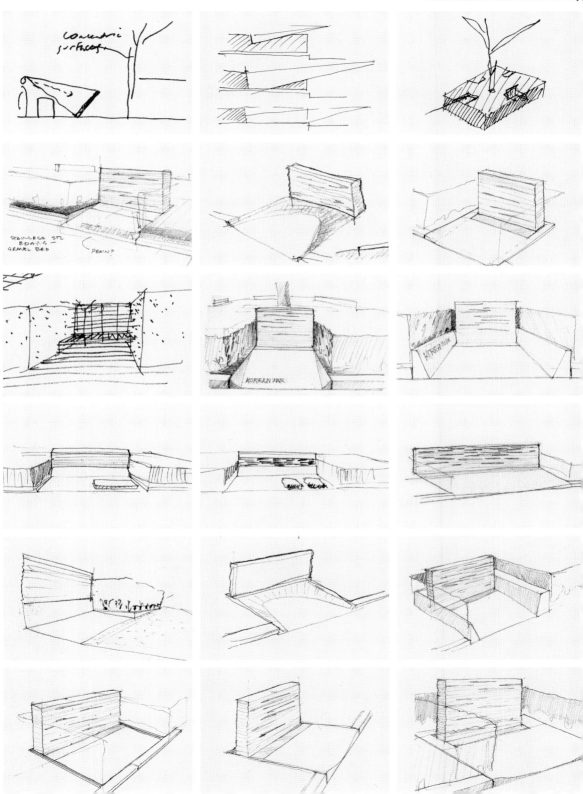

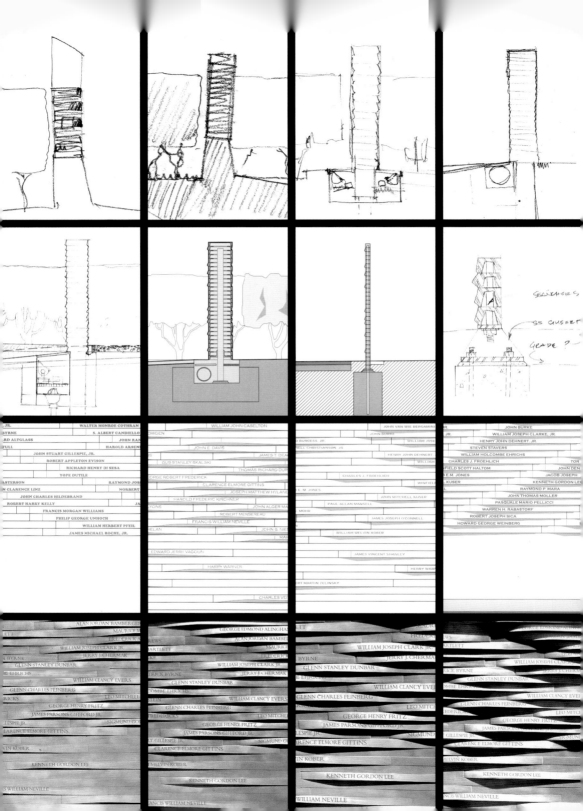

Detail section of typical memorial wall and hedge. Post-tensioned stainless steel rods are threaded through the center of the wall to connect the bricks to each other and to the ground.

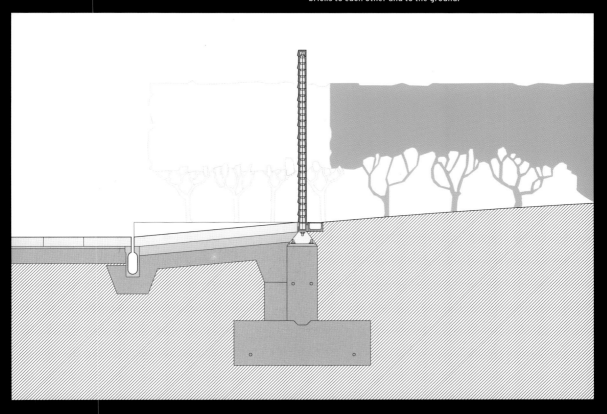

Typical brick plan, sections, and elevation

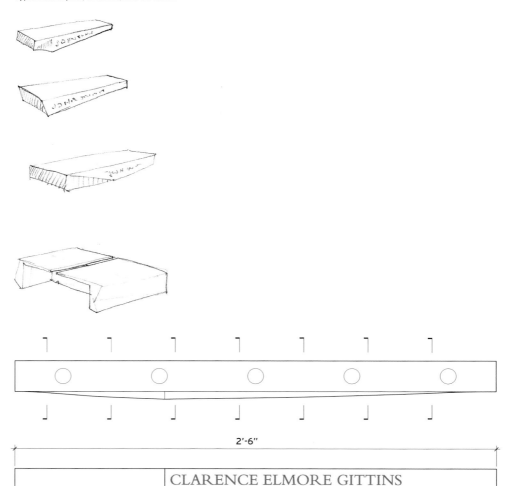

2'-6"

CLARENCE ELMORE GITTINS

architecture research office

The Daily Practice of Collaboration[1]

Guy Nordenson

ARCHITECTURE RESEARCH OFFICE (ARO) has, like many of its contemporaries, chosen to call itself something other than its partners' names. So far the media has not denied them this, as it has with Rem Koolhaas's OMA and Renzo Piano's Building Workshop. ARO shares with these, and with Steven Holl's practice, where Stephen Cassell and Adam Yarinsky worked and met (and where I met and worked with them in the mid-1980s), a commitment to the concept of "design research."

The term "research" is polemical and problematic. It is based on collaboration and empiricism. In positive terms, it appeals to the scientific method, finding ways to test concepts and hypotheses visually, quantitatively, and conceptually. As the English artist Michael Baldwin wrote of the work of Ian Burn and Mel Ramsden,

> Collaboration . . . was not a kind of working-togetherism. It was a matter of destroying the silence of beholding with talk and puzzles, and a forcing any and every piece of artistic "work" out of its need for incorrigibility and into the form of an essay.[2]

In negative terms, it is opposed to the creationist concept of the "Author-God." Which is not to say that the use of a formal language is entirely lost, but rather that aspects other than the surface appearance are considered in the conceptual development and end result.

Memory plays an important part in this work, having the effect of "downplaying the role of the imagination as it is usually conceived: as the expression of individual subjectivity."[3] There is a narrative structure to ARO's work, both in conception and in execution, and it has an important democratic character to it. As in any craft-based practice (in the tradition of Mies and Wright, not Le Corbusier), what Peter Rice called the "*trace de la main*" and Marc Mimram the "*faire à repenser*"[4] enters

93

the picture, as the energetic participation of collaborators is encouraged. This can, but does not necessarily, work against abstraction.

Of the projects included in this book, the one I had most to do with was the SoHo Loft glass stair. The premise ARO and I developed in our earliest discussion was to find a way to cantilever the stair treads from a vertical plane of glass. After a few failed design tests using thick or double glass layer walls, I suggested using a version of what the British call "cantilever" stairs,[5] a concept originally developed in Renaissance Italy[6] and best exemplified by Palladio's stair at the Accademia in Venice. The concept is to actually overcome the low resistance of stone to tension stresses caused through bending by eliminating the cantilever bending of each projecting tread. This is achieved by interlocking it with the treads above and below, which allows each tread to rest on the lower one and for the load to cascade to the bottom. The resulting torsion on each tread can be resisted by the stone and its anchorage to the wall. Thus the cantilever stair becomes in fact anticantilever. The glass stair in the SoHo Loft adapted this concept, using steel risers that are connected to a glass wall and interlocking them with aluminum plate treads to achieve the cascading. The glass wall carries the remaining load that does not cascade down, and the riser torsion.

The project is conceptual, starting with the cantilever paradox and playing on interdependence. There are a number of clues in the stair (the pin connecting the top tread in a slot and the free riser at the bottom, e.g.) that are legible (barely) to an engineer as puzzles. And there are the machine-crafted elements, especially at the glass-to-riser connection, that are clearly far from mass-produced. What makes the result strong is, I think, that it is anything but retinal. This may also make it less appealing to the contemporary eye.

Robert Smithson said, "look at any *word* long enough and you will see it open up into a series of faults, into a terrain of particles each containing its own void."[7]

We need to understand that the same is true for buildings. In some cases, critical analysis can reveal underlying social and economic structures, and their interplay with appearance (as in the work commissioned over the years by Disney, or in the neo-Gothic skin jobs of postmodernism). In other cases, it reveals the poetic interplay of all the parts, particulars, and collaborators, as it does in good movies, and in some works of Gordon Bunshaft (Beinecke Library) and Louis Kahn (Kimbell Art Museum).[8] ARO does not have a style, nor have they engaged much with the contemporary polemics of architecture. They are focusing on the processes and facts of making, and I think, will, with things if not words, change our experiences for the better.

1. After Gerhard Richter's "the daily practice of painting." Gerhard Richter, quoted in Gerhard Richter, "Forty Years of Painting" exhibition brochure, Museum of Modern Art, New York, 2002.

2. Charles Green, *The Third Hand—Collaboration in Art from Conceptualism to Postmodernism* (Minneapolis: University of Minnesota Press, 2001), 55.

3. Ibid., 97.

4. See Françoise Fromonot, *Marc Mimram: Solferino Bridge Paris* (Basel: Birkhäuser Verlag, 2001).

5. Sam Price, "Cantilever Staircases," *Arq* 1 (Spring 1996): 76–87.

6. Probably the first instance of this is the stair in the towers of the Palazzo Ducale in Urbino, built around the 1460s to the design of Luciano Laurana.

7. Jack Flam, ed., *Robert Smithson: The Collected Writings* (Berkeley: University of California Press, 1996), 107.

8. Guy Nordenson, "The Lineage of Structure and The Kimbell Art Museum," *Lotus International* (1998), 28–47.

THIS RESIDENTIAL LOFT is an interior landscape animated by daylight. The seven-thousand-square-foot project occupies the upper floors and roof of a nineteenth-century warehouse in the SoHo neighborhood of Manhattan. The very large floor area, with its ample daylight and views of the skyline in several directions, emits a generous feeling of openness and creates a strong connec-

SoHo Loft, NEW YORK, NEW YORK

tion between inside and outside. These qualities, coupled with the client's love of the outdoors and his desire for a place for entertaining large groups of people, formed the basis of the design.

Natural light defines the organization, ambiance, and detailing of the project. This exploration of light is part of a spatial strategy to maximize the open area of the loft. Diagonal lines of sight make the limits of the building envelope visible. The eye is also directed to views above, below, and beyond the existing space. The design balances this overall visual openness by creating smaller-scaled spaces for specific activities, making roomlike limits to different areas through planes of various materials. These ma-

terials, selected and detailed for their color, texture, reflectivity, and transparency, give a distinct character to each activity.

The functional program of the loft and the client's life are organized by the path of daylight in response to the daily and seasonal cycles of the sun. The master bedroom receives morning light from the east. The kitchen, dining, living, and, finally, the library space receive light progressively during the day, as the sun swings around to the west. The color, intensity, and movement of light are reinforced by the qualities of the materials used for the intimate areas within the open floor plan. These materials also give particular characteristics to different program areas. Large panels of sandblasted glass partially enclose the master bedroom, catching and amplifying the light entering from the skylight above. A blue Bahia granite wall subdivides the kitchen and dining area, and fills the interior with brilliant color. A wool and silk carpet appears like a "lawn," anchoring the seating group within the very large living area.

Roof plan

1   Roof deck
2   Stair vestibule
3   Roof terrace

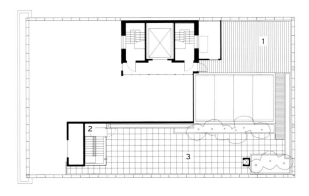

Seventh-floor plan

1   Entry hall
2   Light court
3   Dining room
4   Kitchen
5   Living room
6   Library
7   Master bedroom
8   Master bathroom
9   Dressing room

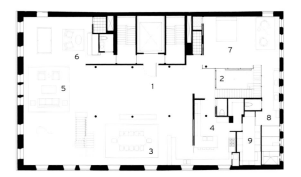

Sixth-floor plan

1   Light court
2   Guest bedroom
3   Office
4   Laundry
5   Media room
6   Bedroom
7   Study

0'   10'

The warm red bubinga wood of the library cabinetry accentuates the color of the setting sun. Throughout the space, highly figured rift and quartered oak flooring is laid in an angular pattern so that daylight strikes the wood perpendicularly to bring out its special markings. In each case, the materials are used in their largest practical sizes so that their texture, color, and pattern are the ornament for the space, creating a continuously changing atmosphere.

A cascading glass-supported stair, designed in collaboration with Guy Nordenson and Associates structural engineers, is a prominent element on the main floor of the loft, providing access to the roof garden and dividing the living and dining areas. Floor-to-ceiling sheets of laminated glass, together with stainless steel risers and aluminum subtreads, were configured to provide structural stability while maximizing visual lightness. The glass stair embodies the strategy, developed throughout the loft, of connecting the experience of the space with the passage of light through it.

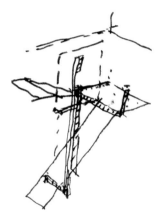

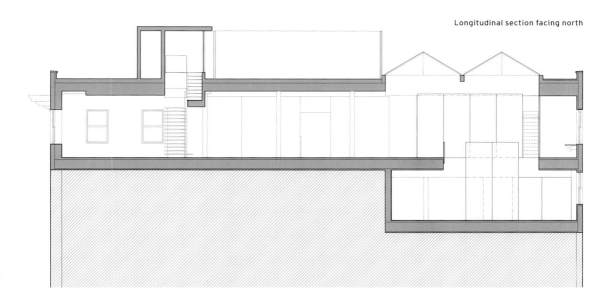

Longitudinal section facing north

Natural light diagram

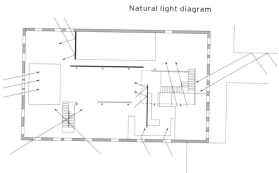

Pattern studies of blue Bahia granite

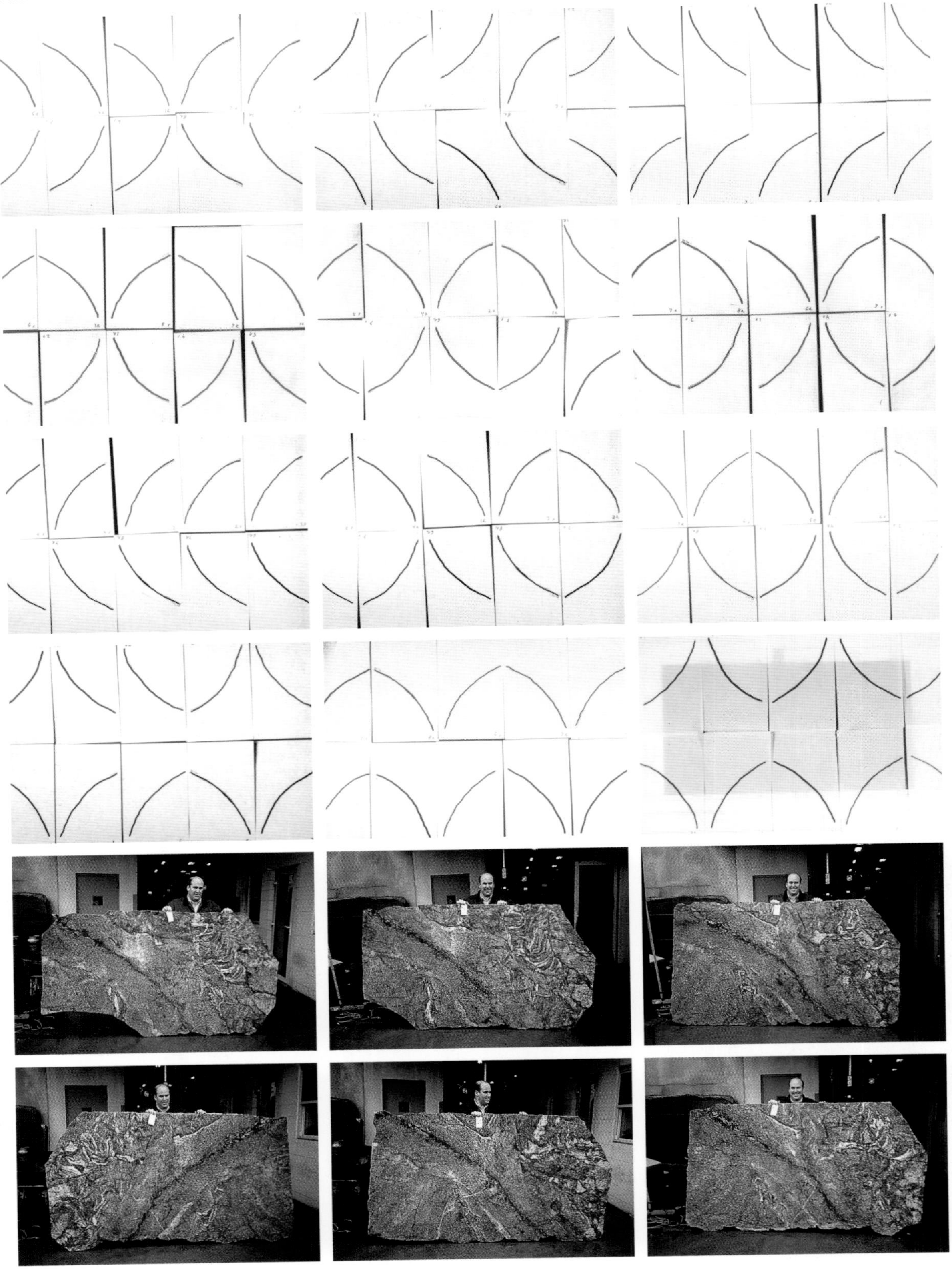

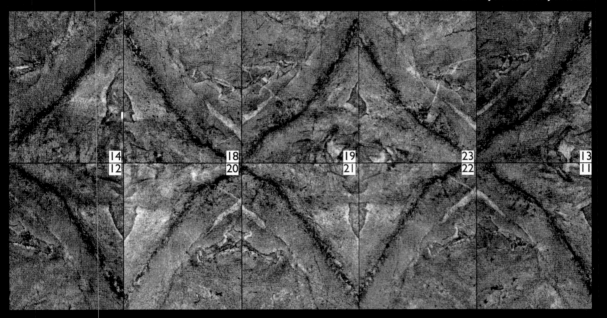

Kitchen

Master bathroom

opposite: Detail of sliding slate panel
at window in master bathroom

106

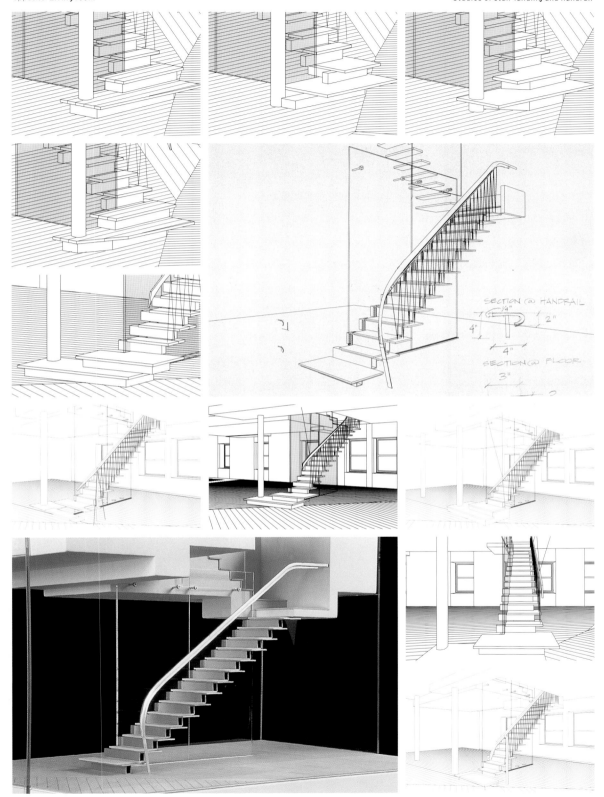

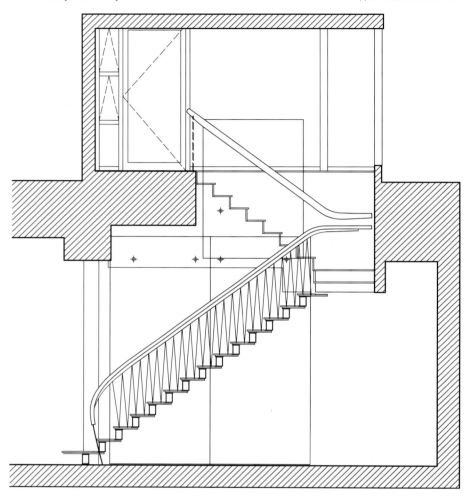

The cascading stair is made of stainless steel tube risers connected by milled aluminum subtreads. The risers attach to large panels of one-and-a-half-inch-thick laminated glass with milled aluminum U-brackets and Delrin wedges. Oak treads are affixed to each sub-tread. Although the stair appears to be cantilevered from the glass, the glass resists only torsional forces, and the load on the stair is supported by the floor. To determine the maximum allowable load on the glass, stress tests were first modeled on the computer and then verified in a full-size mock-up.

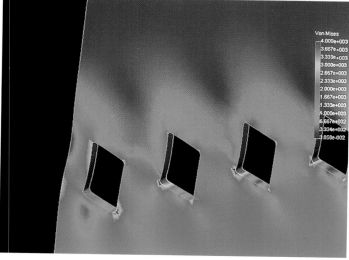

THIS FLAGSHIP STORE AND SPA for a new line of skin care products is located on a busy street in midtown Manhattan. The client wanted the store to act as a beacon for the introduction of their products. The design is therefore a physical elaboration of the product's qualities, a sensory experience imparting the soothing, relaxing, and calm feeling of being outdoors.

ear shapes, these forms create a continuity of space that encourages exploration throughout the interior. Three cylindrical spa cabins float in plan, blurring the boundary between the store and spa areas. To preserve this openness, the service rooms were located along the south edge of the 1,500-square-foot area. Storage and office functions are below the street level.

Qiora Store and Spa, NEW YORK, NEW YORK

Starting with this idea, the emerging language of forms, materials, and lighting created a warm, glowing landscape that is visually open to the exterior. The interior's primary material is light.

The store, located at the front of the space, presents small groupings of the product, whose elegant packaging provides the space with color, scale, and detail. The day spa, which consists of three massage cabins, a lounge, showers, and changing areas, is situated at the rear. The twenty-foot-high ceiling and the large windows establish an open, expansive atmosphere that underlies the entire design strategy. Maximizing the perceived size of the space by using curvilin-

The materials were selected and detailed to reinforce the primary perception of light without the use of extraneous detail, in order to make a quiet context for this experience. The floor is white poured epoxy, a seamless reflective surface that enhances the general glow. All of the walls are veiled in translucent organza fabric panels that hang from the ceiling, requiring few supporting elements. The panels have no seams as their width matches the maximum available width of the fabric. As visitors circulate through the space, layers of fabric panels continually reconfigure collages of color and light. In the store area, the fabric creates soft boundaries between the consultation

architecture research office

and the reception areas. In the spa, fabric shrouds the more intimate spaces of the lounge and cabins. The walls of the cabins are opaque and lined with Ultrasuede, creating a soft and quiet place for relaxation. The shower floors and walls are clad in large sheets of warm white acrylic.

The entire space is illuminated by fabric-diffused fluorescent lighting located on the perimeter walls without visible distracting light fixtures. A computer-controlled dimming system modulates the light between warm and cool shades to create the sensation of daylight and a radiant glow on the skin. This results in a subtle, continuously shifting color of light. As the quality of light changes, it gives a similar effect to that of a cloud passing in front of the sun. This gradual transformation of light changes the perception of the space over time, reinforcing its connection to the outdoors. Extending this play of light further, the products are simultaneously displayed and illuminated as they rest on display fixtures that are lit with fiber optic uplights. These lights cycle through shades of white during the day and blue at night. During the day, the brightness of the interior connects the space to the street, inviting exploration from passersby. At night, the store acts as a lantern to the city.

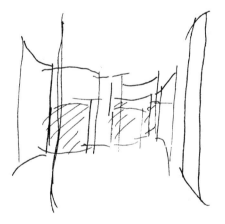

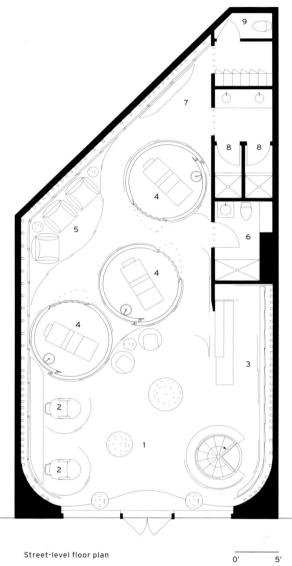

Street-level floor plan

1   Retail area

2   Consultation area

3   Cash/Wrap area

4   Spa cabin

5   Lounge

6   Men's bathroom

7   Women's dressing area

8   Shower

9   Lavatory

0'   5'

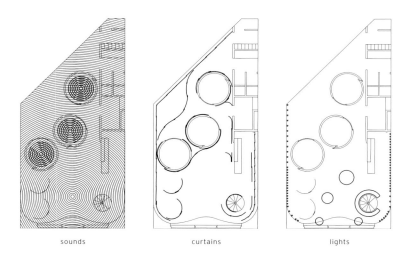

sounds   curtains   lights

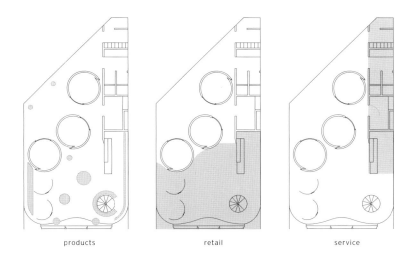

products   retail   service

121

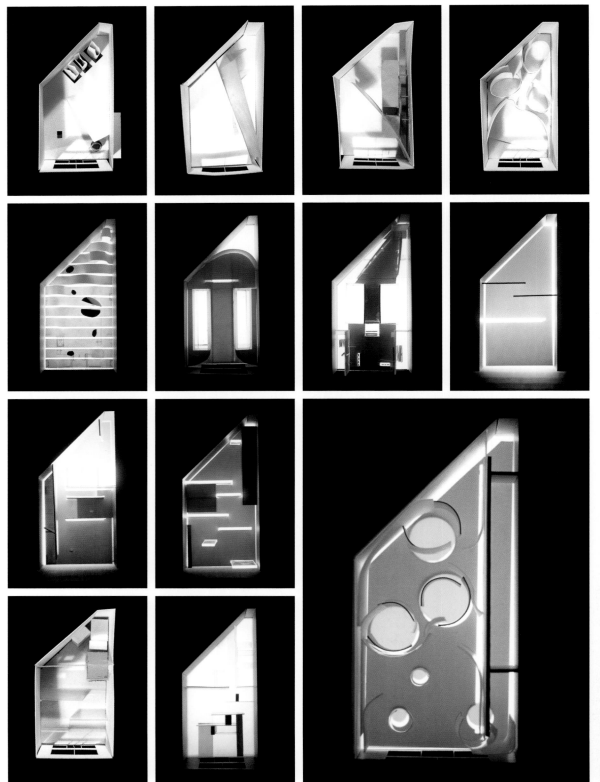

Spa cabin plan

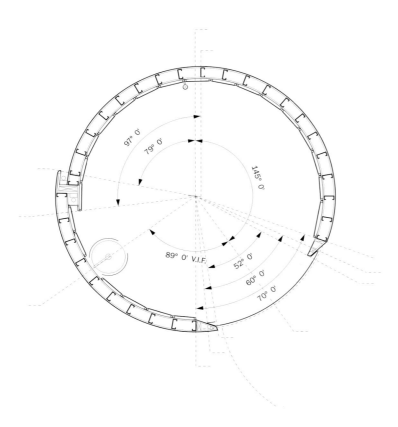

97° 0'

79° 0'

145° 0'

89° 0' V.I.F.

52° 0'

60° 0'

70° 0'

Perspective studies of the overlapping curtains and display fixtures

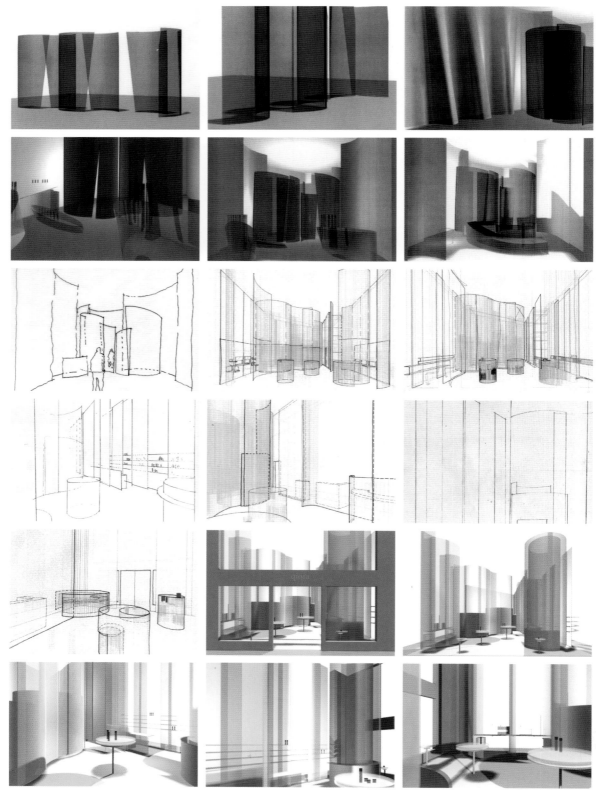

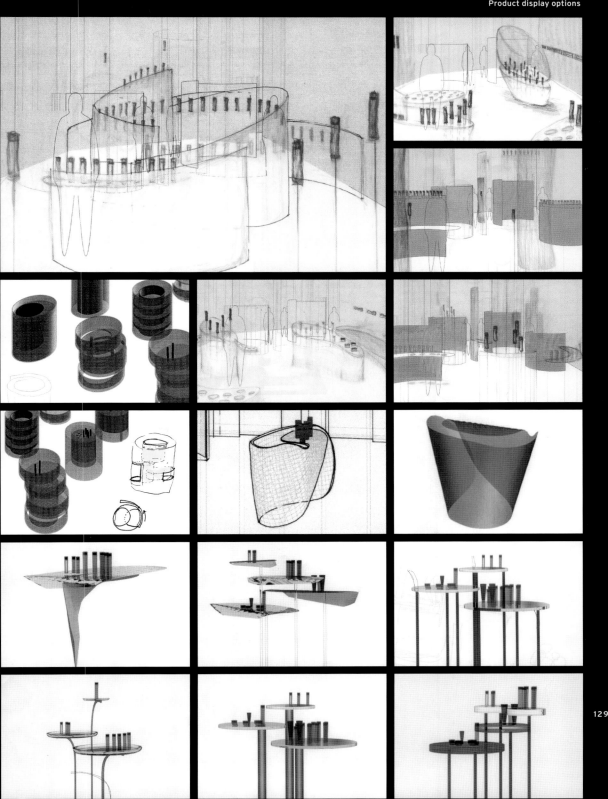

Consultation area

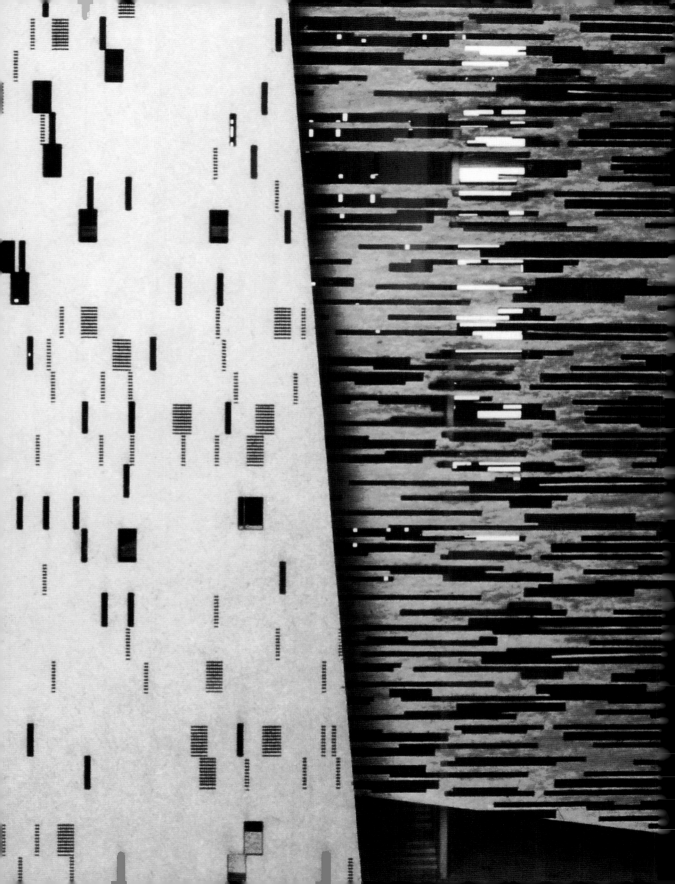

THE DESIGN FOR THE 90,000-square-foot Museum of Art and Technology, located in the new arts district in Chelsea on the west side of Manhattan, was developed for a competition. ARO's competition entry envisaged the museum as a construction of two linked towers, each defined by a highly articulated enclosing skin. The three basic components of the museum, education, production, and exhibition, are grouped into these two towers. The education section is located in the west tower while the exhibition and production sections are found in the east tower.

The programs located in the education tower (which includes classrooms, offices, and a library) share several qualities: they are distinct from the public museum spaces, they have fixed program requirements, and they benefit from daylight. In contrast, the space allocated for the exhibition and the production of art is highly flexible and undifferentiated. This accommodates both the diversity of new media art and the ever-changing technological needs related to its creation and display. The production spaces are designed so that they can be constantly relocated and reconfigured, depending on the museum's current needs and the requirements of the changing technology. These spaces, which are either adjacent to or hanging above the double-height exhibition spaces, are connected to the education tower through a private circulation spine that is formed between the two skins of the building.

The two towers are each contained within a skin that controls daylight, views, and movement. The image of the museum is defined by the qualities of these skins and their dynamic interaction. The skin for the exhibition/production area is structural to permit a column-free interior space and is wired for data distribution to enable the flexible configuration of interior space. It is composed of a series of apertures that control natural light to facilitate the exhibition of projected images and other forms of new media art. In contrast, the education block requires more daylight and is enclosed within a more open envelope. The horizontal openings

Eyebeam Museum of Art and Technology, NEW YORK, NEW YORK

provide panoramic views of the Hudson and mask the appearance of multiple stacked floors to create a unified exterior expression.

The two skins interlock, creating a 140-foot-tall vertical gallery, an expression of the overlapping missions of the museum. The design blurs the boundaries between making and viewing new media art, reflecting the fundamentally interactive nature of the art as well as the pragmatic requirements of the museum. The gallery is a darkened void designed for the presentation of certain types of digital art such as projected still and moving images. It is traversed by means of a moving platform that connects the theater, the lobby, the exhibition areas, and the rooftop restaurant and terraces, and serves as the public's primary means of circulation through the building. Diagonal views across the vertical gallery intensify the interaction between the different parts of the museum and unite the building into one spatial experience. At night, the vertical gallery visually connects the interior with the exterior, glowing with projected light as it gives glimpses of the museum's contents to passing pedestrians and automotive traffic along the West Side Highway.

architecture research office

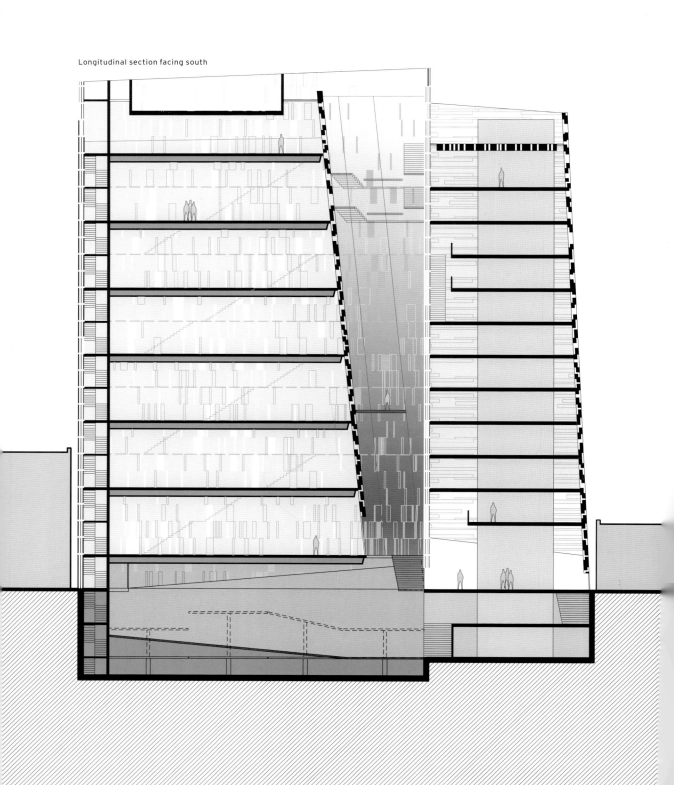

Longitudinal section facing south

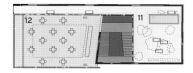

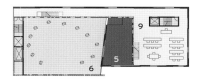

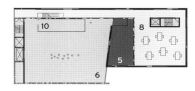

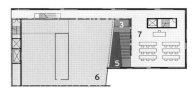

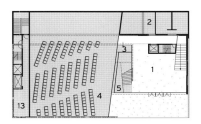

Floor plans

0'   40'

1   Lobby
2   Reception
3   Moving platform
4   Theater/Performance space
5   Exhibition
6   Exhibition/Production
7   Classrooms
8   Offices
9   Library
10 Shared computer lab (Production)
11 Roof terrace
12 Cafe
13 Tenant/Freight entrance

Plan and section options

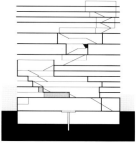

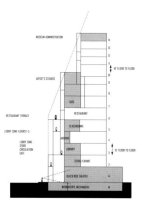

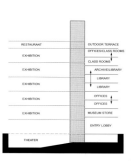

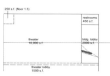

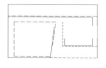

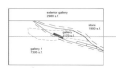

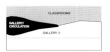

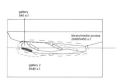

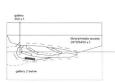

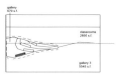

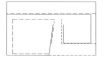

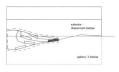

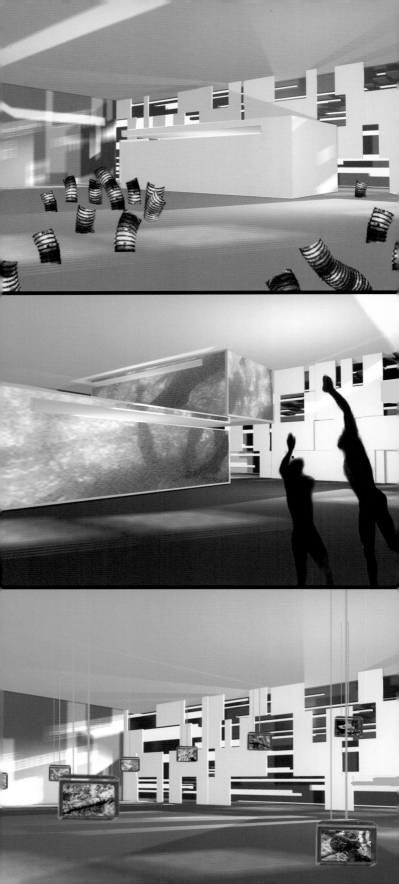

Detail of the exhibition / production skin

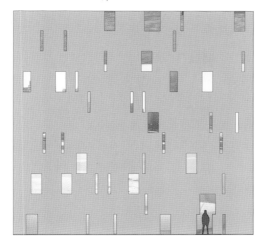

Detail of the education skin

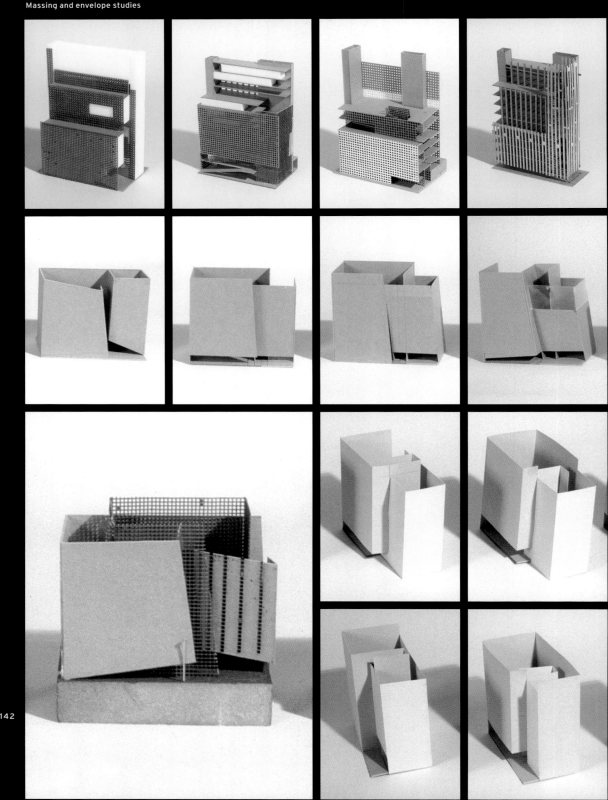

142

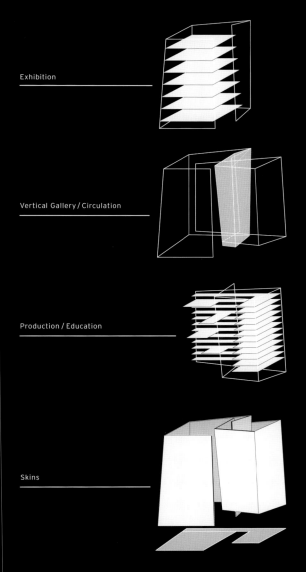

Exhibition

Vertical Gallery / Circulation

Production / Education

Skins

143

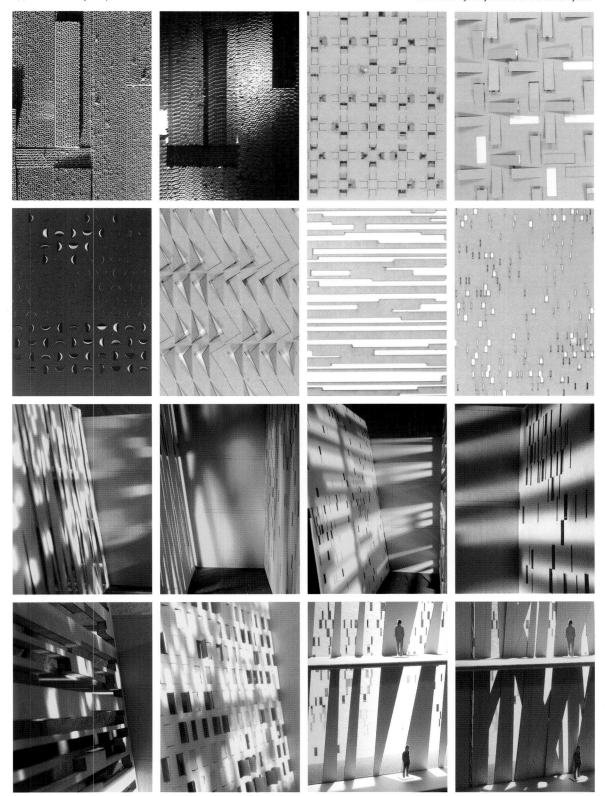

147

Just Design

Philip Nobel

A STRANGE THING HAPPENS when Adam Yarinsky and Stephen Cassell describe the work of ARO. They talk about the utility of limits—temporal and financial—and they celebrate "simultaneity," which they have defined as "the specific economic and social and material context of each project in the real world." They use terms like "experimentation" and "intensity," but you will search in vain for overwrought drawings. They speak openly about using intuition to solve problems. Listening to them, it is hard not to interrupt at some point (as a student once did at a lecture) and ask, "Isn't this just *design*?"

ARO's is a critical practice, but of a rare type: it is not driven by imported theory—the model for experimental architecture with which we are all most familiar, with its equally familiar pitfalls of inscrutability and irrelevance. As Cassell sometimes says, "We are jargon-free architects," and he says it in a way that implies more than the use of simple language. Architecture has gotten to a point where its basic processes have been considered from so many oblique angles that to face them head-on—to embrace architecture as architecture—can be a revolutionary position. The questions that ARO brings to bear on the design process are architecture's own questions: about people (Who's using this thing? How much can they spend?), materials (How heavy is it? Will it bend?), and experience (What is the light doing? What is that space like?). And when they get to the stickiest question—What should it look like?—they usually do not have an answer; they approach each project as a case study in its own possibilities, free of a priori stylistic assumptions.

The simple investigation of the wall, that freighted architectural device, is one place to gauge the effects of ARO's strategically delimited process. Where others might "question the wall" by deforming it or doing away with it altogether, ARO tends to work with the subjects of its critique, looking for subtle, tactical advances. In the Modular Wall project from the mid-1990s, they invented a system that used standard-dimension plywood to create a new kind of flexible partition. It was clearly refined with an eye for effect, but ARO's research was driven by a primal curiosity about what plywood could do. There is a touch of Louis Kahn's material mysticism there: if you were to ask plywood what it wanted to be, it might answer "a bent, slotted partition." In the Courtyard Fence (1995) they puzzled through the responsibilities of an urbane street wall, detailing dignity into sheet steel. In the Colorado House (1999) they developed patterned Cor-Ten scales to put the house into a soft dissonance with the landscape. This was an efficient contextual response in ARO's inclusive definition: the rusting steel references local mine-head structures, breaks the monolithic planes of the house, ties it to the ferrous outcrops of the land, and reflects the inherent *urbs in rus* luxury of the commission; it is clear that ARO used Cor-Ten in part because that particular micromarket would bear it. In the enormous SoHo Loft (1999) they likewise set a decadent wall of blue Bahia granite into a dialogue with humbler materials chosen to amplify the specificity of that project—taking into account everything from the budget to the changing angles of the light. If they do decide to move past reliance on planar walls, they will know what they are leaving behind. And why.

Architects' own point-by-point dissection of their practice has brought the profession to a moment when a radical stand can be made at its own front door: architects should design. ARO is taking that stand by unabashedly pursuing design in its intuitive, incremental, bedrock sense—not to work through intellectual or artistic kinks at a client's expense, not to churn out dim solutions to banal problems, but to find the right forms that ask the right questions in the right place. It is a simple and inexhaustible mandate. Given a specific climate of resources—financial and material, social and cultural—what is possible here? And what is good? Another aspect of ARO's quiet radicalism is that they do not apologize for employing taste. The fear of authorship, that vestige of the scientism that is at the core of the modernist revision of building, has no place in their practice. But neither do they dress their work in deliberate formalism, artistic ideas forced on to a set of conditions alien from their inception.

For all architects, a project begins with a terrible void: there is this empty space and there is the world, and somehow, through erudition, luck, and material magic, the designer is expected to make something in it—something useful, meaningful, lasting, stirring, and quick. It is understandable that some architects—those who have defined their field away from the degree-zero concerns that ARO pursues— would look elsewhere for a way past the fear of a blank slate. It would not be hard to classify all architects by the routes they take around this problem, the particular mirage they trust to force a first decision; some choose familiar or dazzling form, others a favorite idea, usually borrowed. ARO tends to look at the world in its uncomfortable complexity. The project description that the office sent out for the US Armed Forces Recruiting Station (1999) includes a flow chart of the path taken for each design decision through the dozens of federal, state, and local bureaucracies that had a say in the project. It is not a disclaimer: it is a frank and telling revelation of what they considered important in the design, the real and somewhat banal forces that shaped the project and that it aspires to transcend. They did not dodge them and they did not try to cover them up; they incorporated them into the messy job of designing a real thing in an imperfect world. Of course, this is also a useful mirage, or a superstition, or a crutch—this habit of accepting complexity and responding to it with architecture's native rules. But it seems like the right delusion: the one that lies the least.

Project Listing and Credits

THOMPSON STREET APARTMENT
NEW YORK, NEW YORK
1994

A suspended steel stair connects a new pent-
house to the top floor of an existing nineteenth-
century warehouse building.

FLOOR AREA: 5,000 square feet
ARO TEAM: Stephen Cassell, Tom Jenkinson,
Adam Yarinsky; Neil Garrioch, design team

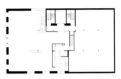

HEAD START PROTOTYPE BUILDINGS
VARIOUS LOCATIONS
1994

Two interlocking L-shaped wings define a central
space that functions as both a meeting hall and
a play area. The wings can be reconfigured in
response to different sites.

FLOOR AREA: 5,000 square feet
ARO TEAM: Stephen Cassell, Adam Yarinsky;
Brenda Edgar, project architect

HOPALONG CASSIDY: KING OF
THE LICENSED COWBOYS
Exhibition Installation
AMERICAN MUSEUM OF THE MOVING IMAGE,
NEW YORK, NEW YORK
1994

A modular wall system of pegboard and inset
Plexiglas cases houses more than seven hundred
objects related to television's first cowboy hero.

FLOOR AREA: 1,200 square feet
ARO TEAM: Stephen Cassell, Adam Yarinsky;
Monica Rivera, project architect; Elena Cannon,
Brenda Edgar, design team
EXHIBITION CONSULTANT: Karen Meyerhoff
FABRICATOR: Peter Hamburger

TRINA SHOWROOM AND OFFICES
NEW YORK, NEW YORK
1994-95

A fabric ceiling system, manufactured by the
client's handbag factory, enabled this low-budget
renovation to be occupied immediately.

FLOOR AREA: 1,500 square feet
ARO TEAM: Stephen Cassell, Adam Yarinsky;
Monica Rivera, project architect

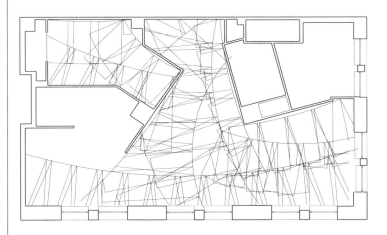

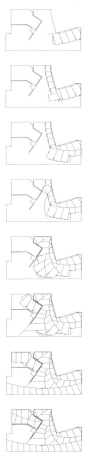

PROTOTYPE SCIENCE AND TECHNOLOGY PARK
1994

Intended to develop the science literacy of urban
youth, this educational facility is interconnected
with a public park. Prefabricated building parts
define a central greenhouse space and can be
reconfigured to adapt to specific sites.

FLOOR AREA: 50,000 square feet
PROJECT CONCEPT AND EXHIBITION DESIGN:
Edwin Schlossberg Incorporated
ARO TEAM: Stephen Cassell, Adam Yarinsky;
Martin Cox, Colleen Hindarto, Youngim Kim,
Sheldon Preston, Monica Rivera, design team

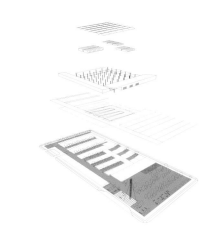

SCULPTURE GALLERY AND COURTYARD FENCE
NEW YORK, NEW YORK
1994-95

The gallery is simply designed with polished concrete floors and white walls that frame views into
the sculpture garden. The garden is enclosed by
thin steel panels, which respond to the scale and
rhythm of the streets bordering the corner site.

FLOOR AREA: 3,000 square feet (gallery);
4,000 square feet (exterior)
ARO TEAM: Stephen Cassell, Tom Jenkinson,
Adam Yarinsky; Monica Rivera, project architect
STRUCTURAL ENGINEER: Gilsanz Murray Steficek
CONSTRUCTION MANAGERS: Clark Construction
Corporation (gallery); B & F Building Corporation (fence)

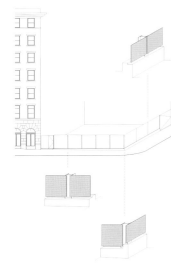

AJAX TELLURIDE OFFICES
TELLURIDE, COLORADO
1994

Designed and built in six weeks, a series of
prefabricated partitions creates work spaces and
a conference room within an existing interior.

FLOOR AREA: 300 square feet
ARO TEAM: Stephen Cassell, Adam Yarinsky

54 THOMPSON STREET LOBBY
NEW YORK, NEW YORK
1994-96

Planes of plate steel and glass define the progression through the lobby and mask the physical limits of the existing narrow space.

FLOOR AREA: 1,200 square feet
ARO TEAM: Stephen Cassell, Tom Jenkinson, Adam Yarinsky
STRUCTURAL ENGINEER: Chris Anastos
CONSTRUCTION MANAGER: B & F Building Corporation

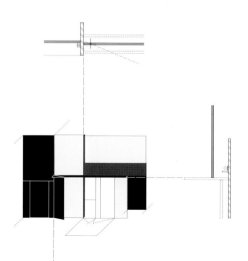

MONKEYS IN ASIAN ART
Exhibition Installation
ASIA SOCIETY, NEW YORK, NEW YORK
1995

Directional lighting and diaphanous fabric strips
create a forest of shadows that forms an animated
backdrop for the display of objects.

FLOOR AREA: 2,000 square feet
ARO TEAM: Stephen Cassell, Adam Yarinsky;
Monica Rivera, Stephen Rogers, design team
EXHIBITION CONSULTANT: Karen Meyerhoff
FABRICATOR: Peter Hamburger

SOHO LOFT
NEW YORK, NEW YORK
1995-99

See pages 96-115

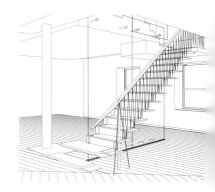

FLOOR AREA: 7,000 square feet (interior);
2,500 square feet (exterior)
ARO TEAM: Stephen Cassell, Adam Yarinsky;
Josh Pulver, project architect;
Elizabeth Alford, Elena Cannon, Reid Freeman,
Tom Jenkinson, Joon Paik, John Quale,
Monica Rivera, Heather Roberge,
Warren Techentin, Wanda Willmore, Greg Yang,
Kim Yao, design team

COLLABORATOR (glass stair structural):
Guy Nordenson and Associates
MECHANICAL ENGINEER: IP Group
STRUCTURAL ENGINEER: Anastos Engineering
LANDSCAPE ARCHITECT: Bruce Kelley/David Varnell
Landscape Architects
LIGHTING: Richard J. Shaver Architectural Lighting
INTERIOR FURNISHING: Lisa Frazar
CONSTRUCTION MANAGER: B & F Building Corporation

CIVICS LESSONS: RECENT NEW YORK
PUBLIC ARCHITECTURE
Exhibition Installation
US CUSTOM HOUSE, NEW YORK, NEW YORK
1996

Located in the rotunda of Cass Gilbert's beaux-
arts US Custom House, the design incorporates
the existing oval desk into a temporary display
system. A new serpentine center wall displays
additional photographs and drawings.

FLOOR AREA: 2,700 square feet
ARO TEAM: Stephen Cassell, Tom Jenkinson,
Adam Yarinsky; Elena Cannon, project architect;
John Quale, Monica Rivera, design team
CURATOR: Lindsay Stamm Shapiro
EXHIBITION CONSULTANT: Karen Meyerhoff
FABRICATORS: Peter Hamburger, Duggal Color Projects

MODULAR WALL, CURVED PLYWOOD
PARTITION SYSTEM
1996

Developing the work of the Ajax Telluride offices,
this project is a system of curved plywood panels
capable of being arranged into varying configurations and sizes.

ARO TEAM: Stephen Cassell, Adam Yarinsky;
Josh Pulver, Monica Rivera, Wendy Weintraub,
design team
FABRICATOR: Reed Karen

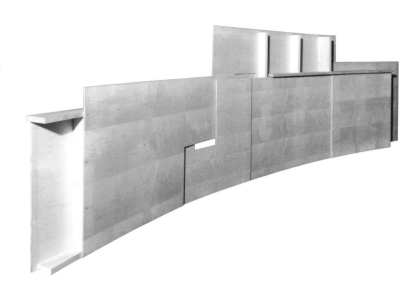

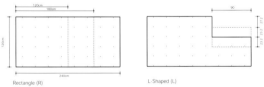

Rectangle (R)

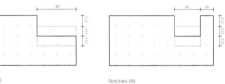

L-Shaped (L)   Notched (N)

	2.4m	2.7m	3.0m	3.3m	3.6m	3.9m	4.2m	4.5m
1.2m								
1.5m								
1.8m								
2.1m								

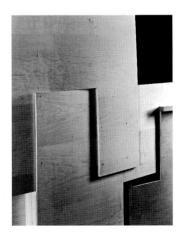

HENRY DREYFUSS: DIRECTING DESIGN
Exhibition Installation
COOPER-HEWITT NATIONAL DESIGN MUSEUM,
NEW YORK, NEW YORK
1996-97

The installation presents case studies of the
work of Henry Dreyfuss, including the telephone
and the round thermostat. Simple white panels
set within the Cooper-Hewitt's Carnegie Mansion
organize the installation and reframe the
familiar objects.

FLOOR AREA: 3,000 square feet
ARO TEAM: Stephen Cassell, Adam Yarinsky;
Josh Pulver, project architect
CURATOR: Russell Flinchum
GRAPHIC DESIGN: Cooper-Hewitt
National Design Museum
FABRICATION: Cooper-Hewitt
National Design Museum

FIFTH AVENUE APARTMENT
NEW YORK, NEW YORK
1996-97

Within the proportions of the existing prewar
apartment, new areas of rich materials add scale,
color, and texture.

FLOOR AREA: 2,000 square feet
ARO TEAM: Stephen Cassell, Tom Jenkinson,
Adam Yarinsky; John Quale, project architect
CONTRACTOR: Alliance Builders

COLORADO HOUSE
TELLURIDE, COLORADO
1996-99

See pages 52-77

FLOOR AREA: 10,000 square feet
ARO TEAM: Stephen Cassell, Adam Yarinsky;
John Quale, project architect; Scott Abrahams,
Matt Azen, Mikel Hoeiland, Jiayur Hsu,
Tom Jenkinson, Niels Nygaard, Monica Rivera,
Martha Skinner, Kim Yao, design team
LANDSCAPE ARCHITECT: Mathews/Nielsen
CONSTRUCTION STRUCTURAL CONSULTANT AND
SEPTIC ENGINEER: Buckhorn Geotech Engineers
MEP ENGINEER: Burggraaf & Associates
LIGHTING: Richard J. Shaver Architectural Lighting
CURTAINS: Mary Bright, Inc.
GENERAL CONTRACTOR: Fortenberry Construction

FLATIRON LOFT
NEW YORK, NEW YORK
1995-96

Located on two floors of a former factory, the
project establishes a variable edge condition
between open spaces and private areas of the
loft through a series of theatrical scrims and
solid sliding panels.

FLOOR AREA: 6,200 square feet
ARO TEAM: Stephen Cassell, Tom Jenkinson,
Adam Yarinsky; Stephen Rogers, project architect;
Timothy Archambault, Joon Paik, Josh Pulver,
John Quale, Monica Rivera, Wanda Willmore,
design team
MECHANICAL ENGINEER: IP Group
GENERAL CONTRACTOR: Up-Rite Construction

3RD FLOOR

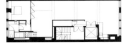

2ND FLOOR

FIFTH AVENUE LOFT
NEW YORK, NEW YORK
1997-98

A cabinet wall defines discrete living areas while
maintaining the perception of open space.

FLOOR AREA: 1,500 square feet
ARO TEAM: Stephen Cassell, Adam Yarinsky;
Josh Pulver, project architect

BIOTHERM PROTOTYPE STORES
MACY'S: SAN FRANCISCO, SAN JOSE,
PLEASANTON, CALIFORNIA
1998

This prototype in-store boutique uses layers of
acrylic, tile, stainless steel, and imagery to dis-
tinguish the space from the larger context of the
department store.

FLOOR AREAS: 500 to 1,500 square feet
ARO TEAM: Stephen Cassell, Adam Yarinsky;
Reid Freeman, project architect;
Scott Abrahams, Alexandra Barker, design team
LIGHTING: Richard J. Shaver Architectural Lighting
CASEWORK CONTRACTOR: Quantum Fine Casework

US ARMED FORCES RECRUITING STATION
TIMES SQUARE, NEW YORK, NEW YORK
1998-99

See pages 12-29

FLOOR AREA: 520 square feet
ARO was design architect/architect of record
and consultant to Parsons Brinckerhoff
ARO TEAM: Stephen Cassell, Adam Yarinsky;
Alan Bruton, project architect; Scott Abrahams,
Eric Ajemian, Jiayur Hsu, Heather Roberge,
design team
MECHANICAL AND STRUCTURAL ENGINEERS:
Parsons Brinckerhoff
GENERAL CONTRACTOR: Element Construction

CAPITAL Z OFFICES
NEW YORK, NEW YORK
1998-2000

The project is located on five floors of an existing
building. Each of the upper floors is arranged
around a central multipurpose space wrapped by
translucent partitions that borrow daylight from
the surrounding private offices.

FLOOR AREA: 27,000 square feet (interior);
4,600 square feet (exterior)
ARO TEAM: Stephen Cassell, Adam Yarinsky;
John Quale, project architect; Kim Yao, project
manager; Erik Ajemian, Matt Azen, Alan Bruton,
Michael Cook, Jiayur Hsu, Josh Pulver, Susan Sloan,
Taunya van der Steen-Mizel, design team
MECHANICAL ENGINEER: IP Group
STRUCTURAL ENGINEER: Selnick/Harwood
Consulting Engineers PC
LANDSCAPE ARCHITECTS: Bruce Kelley/David Varnell
LIGHTING: Kugler Tillotson Associates
AUDIO-VISUAL: Shen Milsom and Wilke
CONSTRUCTION MANAGER: B & F Building Corporation

WESTFIELD HOUSE
WESTFIELD, NEW JERSEY
1997-99

Stone walls connect the landscape and interior
while decreasing the apparent size of the house.
The L-shaped plan and large corner windows ori-
ent rooms toward preferred views.

FLOOR AREA: 10,600 square feet
ARO TEAM: Stephen Cassell, Adam Yarinsky;
Reid Freeman, project architect; Erik Ajemian,
Mikel Hoeiland, Niels Nygaard, Josh Pulver,
Taunya van der Steen-Mizel, Kim Yao,
Innes Yates, design team
LANDSCAPE ARCHITECT: Margie Ruddick
LIGHTING: Richard J. Shaver Architectural Lighting
INTERIOR FURNISHING: Lisa Frazar
CONSTRUCTION MANAGER: Allan Klein

PAPER WALL
NEW YORK, NEW YORK
1999-2000

See pages 30-45

This project was supported by the New York
State Council on the Arts and the Artists
Space Gallery.

ARO TEAM: Stephen Cassell, Adam Yarinsky;
Scott Abrahams, Matt Azen, Alan Bruton,
Jenny Polak, design team
LIGHTING: Richard J. Shaver Architectural Lighting

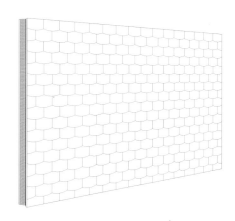

QIORA STORE AND SPA
NEW YORK, NEW YORK
2000

See pages 116-131

FLOOR AREA: 1,500 square feet (street level);
1,500 square feet (below grade)
ARO TEAM: Stephen Cassell, Adam Yarinsky;
Scott Abrahams, project architect; Josh Pulver,
Eunice Seng, Rosalyne Shieh, Kim Yao, design team
DESIGN COLLABORATOR: Aoshi Kudo,
art director, Shiseido
MECHANICAL ENGINEER: Lilker Associates

STRUCTURAL ENGINEER: Selnick/Harwood
Consulting Engineers
LIGHTING: Johnson Schwinghammer Lighting
Consultants, Inc.
CURTAINS: Mary Bright, Inc.
AUDIO-VISUAL: Shen Milsom and Wilke
OWNER'S REPRESENTATIVE: Hiroko Sueyoshi Planners
GENERAL CONTRACTOR: Key International

RAZORFISH OFFICES
PLANNING STUDIES
NEW YORK, NEW YORK
2000

Based on analysis and understanding of both the
conceptual and pragmatic needs of the company,
the project established a program that could
respond to rapid changes and growth.

FLOOR AREA: 200,000 square feet
ARO TEAM: Stephen Cassell, Adam Yarinsky;
Josh Pulver and Kim Yao, project architects;
Matt Azen and Susan Sloan, design team

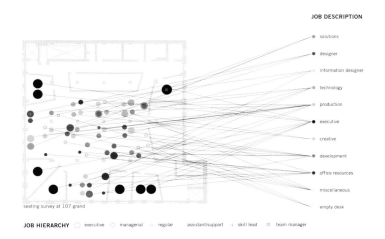

JOB DESCRIPTION

- solutions
- designer
- information designer
- technology
- production
- executive
- creative
- development
- office resources
- miscellaneous
- empty desk

seating survey at 107 grand

JOB HIERARCHY   ○ executive   ○ managerial   ○ regular   assistant/support   skill lead   m team manager

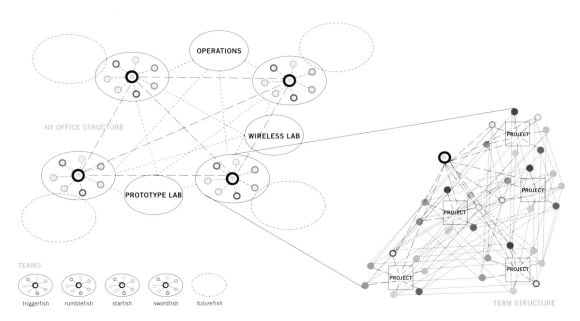

OPERATIONS

NY OFFICE STRUCTURE

WIRELESS LAB

PROTOTYPE LAB

PROJECT
PROJECT
PROJECT
PROJECT
PROJECT

TEAM STRUCTURE

TEAMS

triggerfish   rumblefish   starfish   swordfish   *future*fish

A NETWORKED STRUCTURE

WAR REMEMBRANCE MEMORIAL
COLUMBIA UNIVERSITY, NEW YORK, NEW YORK
2000-

See pages 78-91

AREA: 1,500 square feet
ARO TEAM: Stephen Cassell, Adam Yarinsky;
Ben Fuqua, project architect; Scott Abrahams,
Josh Pulver, Susan Sloan, design team
STRUCTURAL ENGINEER: Leslie E. Robertson Associates
GRAPHIC DESIGN: 2 x 4

PRADA NEW YORK EPICENTER
NEW YORK, NEW YORK
2000-2001

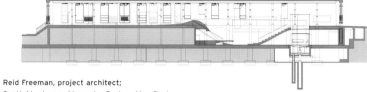

A collaboration between OMA and ARO. Acting as
the architect of record, ARO was responsible for
the detailing and implementation of the project.
The Epicenter is spatially defined by a wave that
drops between floors, housing a retractable stage,
and doubling as bleacher seating and product display.

AREA: 22,000 square feet
DESIGN ARCHITECT: Rem Koolhaas with Office of
Metropolitan Architecture (OMA)
ARO TEAM: Stephen Cassell, Adam Yarinsky;

Reid Freeman, project architect;
Scott Abrahams, Alexandra Barker, Alan Bruton,
Ben Fuqua, Elizabeth Huck, Stephanie Schultze-
Westrum, Susan Sloan, Megumi Tamanaha,
design team
STRUCTURAL ENGINEER: Leslie E. Robertson
Associates
MECHANICAL ENGINEER: Ove Arup & Partners
LIGHTING: Kugler Tillotson Associates
CONSTRUCTION MANAGER: Richter + Ratner
Contracting Corporation

EYEBEAM MUSEUM OF ART AND TECHNOLOGY
Invited Competition
NEW YORK, NEW YORK
2000

See pages 132-147

FLOOR AREA: 90,000 square feet
ARO TEAM: Stephen Cassell, Adam Yarinsky;
Scott Abrahams, Reid Freeman, Ben Fuqua,
Elizabeth Huck, Josh Pulver, Rosalyne Shieh,
Landry Smith, design team
STRUCTURAL ENGINEER: Guy Nordenson
and Associates

GARRISON HOUSE
GARRISON, NEW YORK
1999-2001

This house occupies three levels that step down a
wooded hillside. Designed to reveal the nature of
its construction, the residence uses economical
materials including corrugated aluminum, reinforced
concrete, and engineered lumber.

FLOOR AREA: 2,400 square feet
ARO TEAM: Stephen Cassell, Adam Yarinsky;
Elizabeth Huck, project manager; Scott Abrahams,
Josh Pulver, design team
MECHANICAL AND STRUCTURAL ENGINEER: Allan Klein
CONSTRUCTION MANAGER: B & F Building Corporation

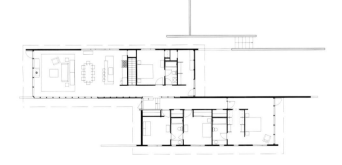

GLASS OF THE AVANT-GARDE:
FROM VIENNA SECESSION TO BAUHAUS
Exhibition Installation
COOPER-HEWITT NATIONAL DESIGN MUSEUM,
NEW YORK, NEW YORK
2001

Shadows of key objects are cast upon
translucent acrylic text panels, revealing their
underlying form.

FLOOR AREA: 3,000 square feet
ARO TEAM: Stephen Cassell, Adam Yarinsky;
Rosalyne Shieh, project architect
CURATORS: Torsten Bröhan, Martin Eidelberg,
Deborah Sampson Shinn
GRAPHIC DESIGN: Cooper-Hewitt
National Design Museum
FABRICATION: Cooper-Hewitt
National Design Museum

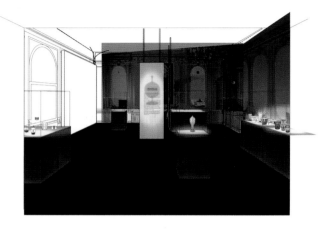

SKIN: SURFACE, SUBSTANCE, AND DESIGN
Exhibition Installation
COOPER-HEWITT NATIONAL DESIGN MUSEUM,
NEW YORK, NEW YORK
2001-02

Undulating curvilinear walls and platforms mediate
between objects and the existing building,
shaping the passage through the exhibition space.

FLOOR AREA: 5,000 square feet
ARO TEAM: Stephen Cassell, Adam Yarinsky;
Elizabeth Huck, project architect;
Rosalyne Shieh, design team
CURATOR: Ellen Lupton
GRAPHIC DESIGN: Cooper-Hewitt
National Design Museum
FABRICATION: Cooper-Hewitt
National Design Museum

SPORTS COLLECTION, DALLAS CENTRAL LIBRARY
DALLAS, TEXAS
2001-02

Stepped like bleachers, this intervention unites
reading, viewing, and gathering, and acts as a
sign to the exterior.

FLOOR AREA: 2,500 square feet
ARO TEAM: Stephen Cassell, Adam Yarinsky;
Ben Fuqua, project architect

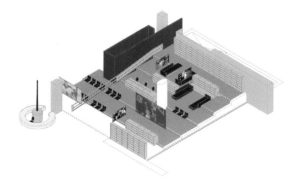

MERCER RESIDENCE
NEW YORK, NEW YORK
2000–

Given its size and program complexity, the design
of this residence is conceived as a hybrid—
combining elements of the country estate, the
urban loft, and the private garden. Two gardens
punctuate a vast open gallery, allowing light
to penetrate through the building, and defining
formal/informal and private/social zones in
the program.

FLOOR AREA: 28,000 square feet
ARO TEAM: Stephen Cassell, Adam Yarinsky;
Kim Yao, project architect; Scott Abrahams,
Matt Azen, Reid Freeman, Ben Fuqua, Josh Pulver,
Eunice Seng, Rosalyne Shieh, Stephanie Schultze-
Westrum, Landry Smith, Megumi Tamanaha,
Jenny Wu, Robert Zeimer, design team
MECHANICAL ENGINEER: Ove Arup & Partners
STRUCTURAL ENGINEER: Leslie E. Robertson Associates
LANDSCAPE ARCHITECT: Ken Smith
Landscape Architect
LIGHTING: Hillman DiBernardo & Associates, Inc.

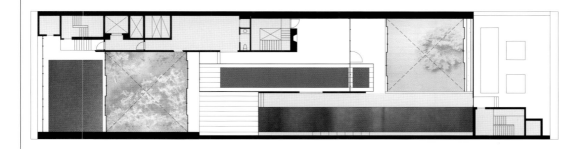

NEW YORK NATURE HOTEL
Commission
COOPER-HEWITT NATIONAL DESIGN MUSEUM,
NEW YORK, NEW YORK
2002

Conceived for the exhibition New Hotels for
Global Nomads, the Nature Hotel is a seasonal
tower made of construction scaffolding, set
among Central Park's trees.

FLOOR AREA: 1,000 square feet
ARO TEAM: Stephen Cassell, Adam Yarinsky;
Ben Fuqua, project architect; Kim Yao, design team

 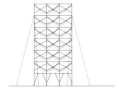

NEW HOTELS FOR GLOBAL NOMADS
Exhibition Installation
COOPER-HEWITT NATIONAL DESIGN MUSEUM,
NEW YORK, NEW YORK
2002

The installation mediates between standard
hotel objects and art works that interpret the
contemporary concept of the hotel.

FLOOR AREA: 9,500 square feet
ARO TEAM: Stephen Cassell, Adam Yarinsky;
Elizabeth Huck, project architect;
Rosalyne Shieh, design team
CURATOR: Donald Albrecht
GRAPHIC DESIGN: Cooper-Hewitt
National Design Museum
FABRICATION: Cooper-Hewitt
National Design Museum

 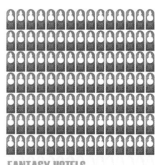  

HOTELS ON THE MOVE   FANTASY HOTELS   URBAN HOT

DESBROSSES LOFT
NEW YORK, NEW YORK
2002-

Selective demolition exposes the existing timber
construction and creates a double-height space
for the living programs of the loft.

FLOOR AREA: 2,400 square feet
ARO TEAM: Stephen Cassell, Adam Yarinsky;
Reid Freeman, senior associate; Eunice Seng and
Jenny Wu, project architects

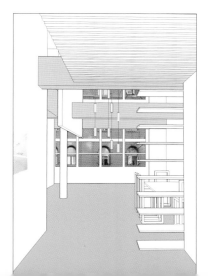

MUSEUM OF MODERN ART/PS 1
WARM-UP INSTALLATION
Invited Competition
LONG ISLAND CITY, NEW YORK
2002

The design is a spatial laboratory that uses thirty
ten-foot-diameter, helium-filled weather balloons,
each with a vertical pull of twenty-five pounds,
to support a web of rope that traverses the existing
triangular gravel sculpture court. The balloons
and rope create an adjustable roof that partially
encloses the space and casts shadows to provide
relief from the summer sun.

AREA: 25,000 square feet
ARO team: Stephen Cassell, Adam Yarinsky;
Ben Fuqua, project architect; Rosalyne Shieh,
design team

WEST STREET HOUSING
NEW YORK, NEW YORK
2002

The design was conceived as part of a larger conceptual proposal for Lower Manhattan and the
World Trade Center site. The changing facade wraps
around to hold together a hybrid typology of
program including retail, lofts, and apartments.

FLOOR AREA: 480,000 square feet
ARO TEAM: Stephen Cassell, Adam Yarinsky;
Ben Fuqua, project architect

MARTHA'S VINEYARD
MARTHA'S VINEYARD, MA
2002–

On a site that offers a singular expansive view
of the ocean, three volumes containing different
programs are arranged to define a series of
exterior spaces.

FLOOR AREA: 2500 square feet
ARO TEAM: Stephen Cassell, Adam Yarinsky;
Josh Pulver, project architect; Eunice Seng and
Rosalyne Shieh, design team

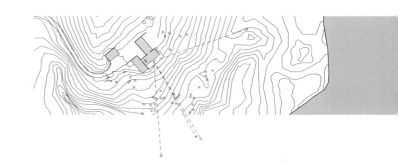

PERMANENT COLLECTION GALLERY
COOPER-HEWITT NATIONAL DESIGN MUSEUM,
NEW YORK, NEW YORK
2002

A display system for the museum's most
precious artifacts sits within a restored interior
of the Carnegie Mansion.

FLOOR AREA: 750 square feet
ARO TEAM: Stephen Cassell, Adam Yarinsky;
Ben Fuqua, project architect

DARWIN MARTIN HOUSE VISITORS CENTER
Invited Competition
BUFFALO, NEW YORK
2002

Serving as an interpretative filter, the design of
the Visitors Center reframes Frank Lloyd Wright's
Martin House, shaping the visitor experience and
amplifying the historical, cultural, and physical
qualities of the place.

FLOOR AREA: 15,000 square feet
ARO TEAM: Stephen Cassell, Adam Yarinsky;
Ben Fuqua, project architect; Reid Freeman,
Beth Huck, Jessica Kung, Mads Moller,
Eunice Seng, Rosalyne Shieh, Landry Smith,
Megumi Tamanaha, design team

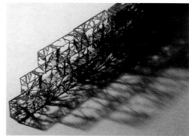

awards

ARO

2001   Finalist, Borromini Award for Young Architects

2001   Emerging Voices
The Architectural League, New York City

2000   Artists' Fellowship, Category of Architecture
Fellowship Program, New York Foundation for the Arts

1998   Independent Project Award
Architecture, Planning and Design Program
New York State Council on the Arts

1996   Young Architects Forum
The Architectural League, New York City

Prada Store

2002   The New York Masterwork Award in the category of Commercial Restoration
The New York Municipal Art Society

Colorado House

2001   American Architecture Award
Chicago Athenaeum: Museum of Architecture and Design

2001   Architecture Award
American Institute of Architects, New York Chapter

Qiora Store and Spa

2002   National Honor Award for Interior Architecture
American Institute of Architects

2001   Design Distinction in Environments
47th I.D. Annual Design Review

2001   Interior Architecture Award
American Institute of Architects, New York Chapter

SoHo Loft

2001   National Honor Award for Interior Architecture
American Institute of Architects

US Armed Forces Recruiting Station, Times Square

2000   Architecture Award
American Institute of Architects, New York Chapter

2000   American Architecture Award
Chicago Athenaeum: Museum of Architecture and Design

2000   Design Distinction in Environments
46th I.D. Annual Design Review

1999   17th Annual Awards for Excellence in Design
Art Commission of the City of New York

1998   Design Award
American Institute of Architects, New York Chapter

Henry Dreyfuss: Directing Design (exhibition)

2000   Federal Design Achievement Award

1998   Selected for the 100 Show
The American Center for Design, Chicago

54 Thompson Street Lobby

1998   Award of Merit
American Institute of Architects, New York State

1997   Design Citation
American Institute of Architects, New York Chapter

exhibitions

2001   Architecture Research Office
       Atlanta Contemporary Art Center, Atlanta, Georgia

2001   Architecture Research Office
       University of Virginia School of Architecture,
       Charlottesville, Virginia

2000   Architecture Research Office: Work
       Princeton University, Princeton, New Jersey

2000   Paper Wall
       Artists Space, New York, New York

1999   Recent Work
       University of Arkansas, Fayetteville, Arizona

1998   Strategy Material Construction
       Syracuse University, Syracuse, New York

1997   Recent Work
       Harvard University Graduate School of Design
       Cambridge, Massachusetts

2002 55 Water Street Plaza Competition
      Urban Center Galleries, New York, New York

2002 What Next for Lower Manhattan Symposium Exhibition
      Venice Biennale, Venice, Italy

2002 New Hotels for Global Nomads Exhibition
      Cooper-Hewitt National Design Museum, New York, New York

2002 PS1 Warm-Up Installation
      Museum of Modern Art Queens, Long Island City, New York

2002 Skin: Surface, Substance, and Design Exhibition
      Cooper-Hewitt National Design Museum, New York, New York

1996 Young Architects Forum Exhibit
      The Architectural League, New York, New York

bibliography

2002   "Architecture Research Office." *Quaderns* No. 232 (January 2002): 112–117; US Armed Forces Recruiting Station.

Carter, Brian, and Anette LeCuyer. *All American—Innovation in American Architecture.* New York: Thames & Hudson, 2002: 13–23; various projects.

Hart, Sara. "A Seismic Meeting of Retail and Architecture." *Architectural Record* 190, no. 2 (February 2002): 84–87; Prada New York Epicenter.

Lupton, Ellen, et al. *Skin: Surface, Substance, and Design.* New York: Princeton Architectural Press, 2002: 160, 212–213; various projects.

McGuire, Penny. "Japanese Lantern." *Architectural Review* 211, no. 1260 (February 2002): 79–81; Qiora Store and Spa.

Vercelloni, Matteo. *Offices for the Digital Age in USA.* Milan: Edizioni L'Archivolto, 2002: 42–55; 54 Thompson Street Lobby, Capital Z Offices.

Vercelloni, Matteo. "Qiora Store." *Interni*, no. 518 (February 2002): 110–113.

Wenz-Gahler, Ingrid. "Qiora Store and Spa: New York." In *Concept Shops.* Stuttgart: Verlagsanstalt Alexander Koch GmbH, 2002: 30–33.

2001   Amelar, Sarah. "Record Interiors." *Architectural Record* 189, no. 9 (September 2001): 113–119; Qiora Store and Spa.

Architecture Research Office. "Paper Wall." *Building Material, Journal of the Architectural Association of Ireland* 7 (September 2001): 24–29.

Architecture Research Office. "Paper Wall, ARO." *Intersight 6, Journal of the School of Architecture and Planning SUNY Buffalo* (March 2001): 21–32.

Balfour, Alan. "Commercial Low Rise." In *World Cities. New York.* New York: John Wiley & Sons, 2001: 98; US Armed Forces Recruiting Station.

Barreneche, Raul. "Design 100: Next!" *Metropolitan Home* 33, no. 2 (March/April 2001): 68; ARO and SoHo Loft.

Fernandez-Galiano, Luis, ed. "Bars Without Stars." *Arquitectura Viva*, no. 76 (January–February 2001): Cover, 50–51; US Armed Forces Recruiting Station.

Korhammer, Justin. "The Experimental Building Practice of Architecture Research Office." *de Architect* 32 (January 2001): 38–43; various projects.

Lewis, Julia. "Quality of Light." *Interior Design* 72, no. 1 (January 2001): 162–168; Capital Z Offices.

Makovsky, Paul. "20 Years of Emerging Voices." *Metropolis* 20, no. 7 (March 2001): 190.

Moonan, Wendy. "Record Houses." *Architectural Record* 189, no. 4 (April 2001): 113–119; Colorado House.

Muschamp, Herbert. "Forget the Shoes, Prada's New Store Stocks Ideas." *New York Times*, (16 December 2001), sect. 9, pp. 1, 6.

Nobel, Philip. "Dance of Veils." *Interior Design* 72, no. 4 (April 2001): 194–197; Qiora Store and Spa.

"Qiora Spa." *I.D. 2001 Design Review* 48, no. 5 (August 2001): 120.

Raggi, Gabriella. "Architectural Research Office." *Casabella*, no. 691 (August 2001): 113–119; US Armed Forces Recruiting Station.

Sirefman, Susanna. *New York*. London: Ellipsis, 2001: 8.16–8.17; US Armed Forces Recruiting Station.

"Two Shops in New York." *Detail* 41, no. 2 (February 2001): 211; Qiora Store and Spa.

Vercelloni, Matteo. "Il segno nel paesaggio." *Interni* 511 (May 2001): 105–111; Colorado House.

Yoshida, Noboyuki, ed. "ARO: Qiora Store and Spa." *A+U*, no. 368 (May 2001): 63–69.

Yoshio Futagawa, ed. "ARO/Garrison House." *Global Architecture Houses, #66/Project 2001*: 15.

2000 Adams, Nicholas. "Sign City: Dalla relazione di progetto." *Casabella*, no. 673/674 (December 1999–January 2000): 32–34; US Armed Forces Recruiting Station.

Bretler, Marc, ed. "Feature ARO." *A+U*, no. 357 (June 2000): 3-112.

Bussel, Abby. "Living Daylight." *Interior Design* 71, no. 2 (February 2000): Cover, 112–121; SoHo Loft.

Lamuniere, Ines. "Tungstènes, Neons, ou Comment 'Devenir Grand.'" *Faces* 48 (Fall 2000): 21–23; US Armed Forces Recruiting Station.

Le Blanc, Sydney. *The Architecture Traveler: 250 Key 20th Century American Buildings*. New York: Whitney Guides, 2000: 250; US Armed Forces Recruiting Station.

Rappaport, Nina. "Armed Forces Recruiting Station, Architecture Research Office." *Architecture* 89, no. 1 (January 2000): 96–101.

Rus, Mayer. "The Building Blocks." *W* 29, issue 10 (October 2000): 238–250; various projects.

Slessor, Catherine. *Contemporary Staircases*. London: Mitchell Beazley, 2000: 26–29; SoHo Loft.

Torre, Stefania della. "Architettura del colore." *Luce* 39, no. 4 (October 2000): 92–100; US Armed Forces Recruiting Station.

"US Armed Forces Recruiting Station, Times Square." *I.D. 2000 Design Review* 47, no. 5 (August 2000): 148.

White, Norval. *AIA Guide to New York, Fourth Edition.* New York: Three Rivers Press, 2000: 109, 258; various projects.

1999 Iovine, Julie V. "This Is Your Life (It's Also Their Art)." *New York Times*, 4 November 1999, F1, F7; SoHo Loft.

Louie, Elaine. "Trade Secrets: Light to Make Walls Dance." *New York Times,* December 9, 1999, F9; Modular Wall.

Nasatir, Judith. "Material Whirl." *Metropolitan Home* 31, no. 5 (September–October 1999): 86–90; Flatiron Loft.

Nobel, Philip. "In the Belly of the Beast." *Metropolis* 18, no. 10 (July 1999): 100–111; various projects.

Uddin, M. Saleh. *Digital Architecture.* New York: McGraw-Hill, 1999: 84–85; Colorado House.

Volkmann, Christian. "Architetti a New York: Avanguardie o retrovie? Una controversia." *Archi*, no. 5 (October 1999): 24–27; various projects.

Yoshio Futagawa, ed. "ARO/Colorado House." *Global Architecture Houses, #59/Project 1999*: 20–21.

1998 Bussel, Abby. "Clean Slate." *Interior Design* 69, no. 9 (July 1998): 82–84; Fifth Avenue Loft.

Hart, Sara. "The Engineer's Hand." *Architecture Magazine* 87, no. 11 (November 1998): 158–162; SoHo Loft.

Rappaport, Nina. "Sightseeing." *db magazine* (September 1998): 101; 54 Thompson Street Lobby.

Rus, Mayer. *Loft.* New York: Monacelli Press, 1998: 122–133; Flatiron Loft.

1997 Bussel, Abby. "Glass Plus." *Interior Design* 67, no. 7 (May 1997): 212–215; 54 Thompson Street Lobby.

Carter, Brian. "Urban Artefacts." *Architectural Review* 202, no. 1209 (November 1997): 86–87; Sculpture Gallery and Courtyard.

Nasatir, Judith. "Water World." *Interior Design* 67 (October 1997): 68; Fifth Avenue Apartment.

Muschamp, Herbert. "Form Follows Function into Ideal Circles." *New York Times*, 28 March 1997, Weekend, pp. 1, 25; Henry Dreyfuss Exhibition.

Rappaport, Nina. "Young Architecture from New York." *Schweizer Ingenieur und Architekt*, no. 48 (November 1997): 4–5; 54 Thompson Street Lobby, Colorado House, Westfield House.

Webb, Michael. "Downtown Perspective." *Architectural Digest* 54, no. 8 (August 1997): 104–109, 166; Flatiron Loft.

1996 Bressi, Todd W. "AIA New York Exhibits Civic Architecture." *Architecture* 85, no. 5 (May 1996): 38; Civics Lessons Exhibition.

Muschamp, Herbert. "Workmanlike Efforts for Society's Nuts and Bolts." *New York Times*, 14 April 1996, p. 36; Civics Lessons Exhibition.

"News: Rising Design Stars." *Architecture* 85, no. 5 (May 1996): 38, 51; 1996 Young Architects' Award.

Yoshio Futagawa, ed. "Loft Apartment, Flatiron District, NY." *Global Architecture Houses, #48/Project 1996*: 12–13.

1995 Waters, Debra. "Architecture Research Office: Emerging Firms Profile." *Oculus* 59, no. 1 (October 1995): 9.

Yoshio Futagawa, ed. "Loft Apartment." *Global Architecture Houses, #45/Project 1995*: 16–17; Thompson Street Apartment.

Princeton Architectural Press, New York
Published by
Princeton Architectural Press
37 East Seventh Street
New York, New York 10003

For a free catalog of books, call 1.800.722.6657
Visit our Web site at www.papress.com.

© 2003 Princeton Architectural Press
All rights reserved
Printed and bound in China
06 05 04 03 5 4 3 2 1 First edition

No part of this book may be used or reproduced in any
manner without written permission from the publisher,
except in the context of reviews.

Every reasonable attempt has been made to identify
owners of copyright. Errors or omissions will be corrected
in subsequent editions.

Publication of this book has been supported by a
grant from the Graham Foundation for Advanced Studies
in the Fine Arts.

Project Editing: Clare Jacobson and Nicola Bednarek
Copy Editing: Nicola Bednarek
Design: Alexa Mulvihill

Special thanks to: Nettie Aljian, Ann Alter, Janet Behning,
Megan Carey, Penny Chu, Russell Fernandez, Mark Lamster,
Nancy Eklund Later, Linda Lee, Jane Sheinman, Katharine
Smalley, Scott Tennent, Jennifer Thompson, and Deb Wood
of Princeton Architectural Press
                                      —Kevin C. Lippert, publisher

ARO would like to thank Matt Azen, Megan Kelly-Sweeney,
Jessica Kung, Mads Moller, Jenny Polak, Landry Smith, and
Kim Yao for their work on this book.

Library of Congress Cataloging-in-Publication Data

Cassell, Stephen.
ARO : Architecture Research Office / Stephen Cassell and
Adam Yarinsky.— 1st ed.
     p. cm. — (Graham Foundation/Princeton Architectural
Press series, new voices in architecture)
Includes bibliographical references.
     ISBN 1-56898-367-0
1. Architecture Research Office. I. Yarinsky, Adam. II.
Architecture Research Office. III. Title. IV. Series.
     NA737.A76 A4 2003
     720'.92'2—dc21   2002011010

PHOTO CREDITS:
US Armed Forces Recruiting Station: David Joseph, except
p. 23 Landry Smith
Colorado House: Paul Warchol, except p. 76-77 Mark Heithoff
Paper Wall: Reid Freeman
Soho Loft: Paul Warchol, except p. 109 Midge Eliasson
Qiora Store and Spa: David Joseph, except p. 124 Reid Freeman
Eyebeam: Reid Freeman
Project Listing and Credits:
Hopalong Cassidy, Trina Showroom, Ajax Telluride Offices,
Monkeys in Asian Art Exhibition, Civic Lessons Exhibition,
and Modular Wall: Ross Muir
Sculpture Gallery: Adam Yarinsky
54 Thompson Street Lobby, Henry Dreyfuss Exhibition,
Colorado House, Flatiron Loft, Capital Z Offices, and
Garrison House: Paul Warchol
Fifth Avenue Loft, US Armed Forces Recruiting Station,
Westfield House, Qiora Store and Spa: David Joseph
Biotherm Prototype Stores: Cesar Rubio
War Remembrance Memorial and Eyebeam: Reid Freeman
Skin: Surface, Substance, and Design Exhibition:
Bill Jacobson